GARDIE

A Shetland house and its people

Drawn by A. M. Horne.

Engraved by D. Havell.

GARDIE HOUSE the RESIDENCE of Wᵐ MOUAT Esqʳ

GARDIE

A Shetland house and its people

Wendy Scott

The Shetland Times Ltd.
Lerwick
2007

First published by The Shetland Times Ltd., 2007.

ISBN 978-1-904746-26-3 (Hardback)
ISBN 978-1-904746-27-0 (Paperback)

A CIP catalogue record for this book is available from the British Library.

Printed and published by
The Shetland Times Ltd.,
Gremista, Lerwick, Shetland,
ZE1 0PX, Scotland.

We have to live inside the history we're given, but must resist, like radicals, being made into mere creatures of a mere era.

Carol Shields *Unless*

CONTENTS

ILLUSTRATIONS

PREFACE

My first memories of Gardie House are of a vast, dark, mysterious place. The faces of unknown men frowned sternly from the walls; one was never warm. Later it happened that I myself came to live there, a circumstance which was to change my life. The house slowly became our home in which all the normal family things happened, and, having other preoccupations, I thought at first very little about its history, of which I was entirely ignorant.

It was only as the children grew up, and began as children do to ask questions, that my own curiosity awakened. Prompted one day by looking out through the original window panes in the drawingroom, where the old glass makes the view across the Sound to Lerwick decidedly wiggly, it struck me that the gentleman in the full wig who lives on the opposite wall of the room must have looked out through those very same wiggly windows. What did he see, I wondered; and from there it was a short step to asking other questions – who were they, the people who were here before us; what happened to them, and, most important of all, what was it like to be alive then.

This book is an attempt to answer some of these questions. Since so many of the people involved were closely connected with wider events in Shetland history, it means trying to understand the ebb and flow of events and trends which affected their own lives, and the lives of others. They and their contemporaries speak for themselves through the documents which have survived. Although some of these are housed in the Shetland Archive in Lerwick, Gardie House is fortunate enough to possess its own, large, collection of papers - personal and business letters, ledgers, accounts and so on – which make up the Gardie House Archive, and this material forms the basis of the book.

Gardie House never existed in a vacuum; the money to build it was earned in the economic circumstances of its day, and to get any sort of picture one must go back well before its building in 1724.

During the 1600's Scottish institutions were imposed upon Shetland, a society still Scandanavian in language, custom and thought, and as yet only partially absorbing the culture which accompanied the geopolitical reality of the mortgaging of the islands by Norway to the Scots crown in 1469. Underpinned by Scots immigration during the 17th century, the pace of change accelerated, signalled by the replacement of Norse nomenclature by Scots. Thus fouds[1] became baillies; Scots law superceded Norse; land holding was legitimised by Scottish legal documents, and the old Norn dialect, gradually dropping out of use, served to enrich the vibrant Scots tongue which overmastered it. Another Scots import, the violin, was so far adopted by Shetlanders as to become one of the prime emblems of their culture, the fiddle music which continues with notable vitality to the present day.

The Scots who came to Shetland were unpopular, as immigrants usually are; they were driven by the prime motivation of immigrants, survival. Some were able men, and some were to have a considerable impact upon their new home.

It was the sea which supported the islands: to Shetlanders a larder, a playground, a highway, and the essential provider of the fish whose export enabled them to buy what the islands could not produce. Every year foreign merchants bartered on the beaches, a system that had gone on time out of mind and was nearly as sure as the annual return of the tirricks (arctic terns) which signals summer in Shetland. But nothing is for ever. By the 1680's there were disquieting signs that the old familiar ways were changing, and it was not clear to islanders how things might turn out.

It was about this time, when thinking men could see trouble ahead, that one man, no longer young, but perhaps only in early middle age, took the decision to leave one island, Unst, and move to another, Bressay. It is with this economic migration, undoubtedly undertaken in hopes of a better life, that the story begins.

---

1   Foud – an official, originally of the Norwegian crown, with prescribed duties including that of collecting taxes.

CHAPTER ONE

MAGNUS HENDERSON

> *Magnus Henderson built the best house in Shetland and above his fortune anno 1724.*
> Thomas Mouat of Garth, Annotated Signatures, 1814.

When the Norse came to Shetland in the ninth century they found a standing stone, ten feet high, on a hill above Bressay Sound. On the level ground nearby a settlement was established, named for its spring of sweet water (Old Norse '*kelda*'). Below it the land falls to shelving grassy banks beside the sea, looking out over the waters of Bressay Sound.

The island of Bressay, curving in a gentle arc opposite the Shetland mainland, forms half of one of the safest anchorages in the North Atlantic. Time out of mind men have come here to fish the rich grounds off the north and east of Shetland, and to lie in for shelter and replenishment of supplies. During the 17th century the Dutch fishing fleet gathered here before beginning a summer's fishing, and traded with islanders in booths along the shore. They needed fresh provisions, the woollen stockings for which local women were famed, and other services too, the kind strongly disapproved of by the Church (trading in Bressay Sound had been forbidden several times owing to associated lawlessness, including drunkenness, theft, prostitution, assault and murder).[1] In the face of official disapproval and occasional enemy action – Lerwick was burnt during the Anglo-Dutch War of 1673 – the little town, scruffy,

1

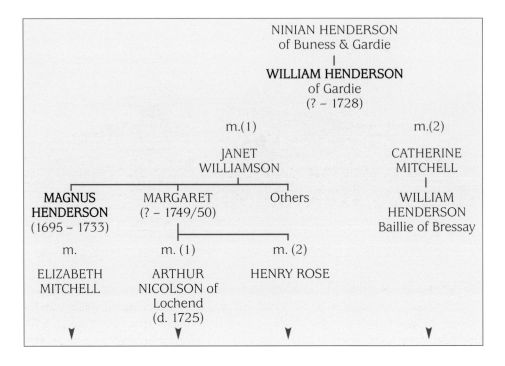

cosmopolitan, commercial, sinful, slowly grew outwards from where it huddled against the walls of its protective – and now ruinous – fort.

It was the commercial importance of Bressay Sound which drew William Henderson to leave his home at Gardie in South Unst and settle on the Bressay shore sometime in the early 1690s. Henderson was one of those who, finding their income from the land inadequate, decided to go into trade, and his new home was conveniently near the hub of activity. He lived on the banks of Keldabister near the home of his business partner, "Skipper" Laurence Williamson, cementing the alliance by marrying Skipper's eldest daughter. Their first son Magnus was born there in 1695.

Laurence Williamson seems to have been an astute character. All his daughters made good marriages, reinforcing and underpinning their father's social and economic alliances in the usual fashion of the times (family ties acted as a kind of insurance for individuals against the vagaries of life). One married the local minister, Hugh Leigh, possibly not a move calculated to promote her happiness (Leigh was suspended by

"Lerwick from the stony hill", showing the sweep of Bressay beyond. © Shetland Museum

the Presbytery in 1702 for beating her),[2] but a judicious one, since Leigh's first wife had been sister to Thomas Gifford of Busta, Chamberlain to the Earl of Morton and probably the most important man in Shetland. If Skipper married his heiress Janet to an Unst man, then the Unst man was probably someone to watch.

William Henderson's date of birth is unknown but he had a charter of lands from his father in 1688 and was a Commissioner of Supply in 1696, 1698 and 1704; in character he was later described as "a respectable honest man of strong natural endowments and good disposition and an exemplary husband and father."[3] His family, of Norwegian descent, had long been settled in Unst, where his great-grandfather, one of the complainers against the arbitrary abuses of Bruce of Cultmalindie in 1575[4] later served as Underfoud of Unst in 1582, and again from 1591-1605. William Henderson took pride in his Norwegian ancestry, and was known as "Gardie", after his Unst property (a custom which long persisted in the landward areas of Shetland). He set out to survive and prosper in a difficult and sometimes hostile world.

William Henderson's Shetland was a testing environment in which to live. If he and his peers were tough, their God was no less tough and the results of things going wrong often disastrous. Shetlanders lived as they had always done, in a cycle of occasional glut and frequent scarcity. Population levels remained low, with hunger at best and famine at worst culling the young, the old, the sick. The 1690s were marked by appalling famine in Scotland; in the isles many staved off starvation by living exclusively on sillocks (young saithe). In 1700 a smallpox epidemic swept though Shetland causing heavy casualties. Thereafter at regular twenty year intervals, major outbreaks took their toll of the rising generation (smallpox is predominantly a killer of the young), and there were many more local outbreaks in addition. It is hardly surprising that the Shetland population remained at best static. Land often lay unused for want of hands to work it.

A generation later the continuing effects of the high mortality rate in Unst were described by an eye witness who, on behalf of Andrew Ross, factor to Lord Morton, "made particular enquiry of the lands tenanted and ley *(unworked)* in Unst Anno 1735 and found near one third part ley.

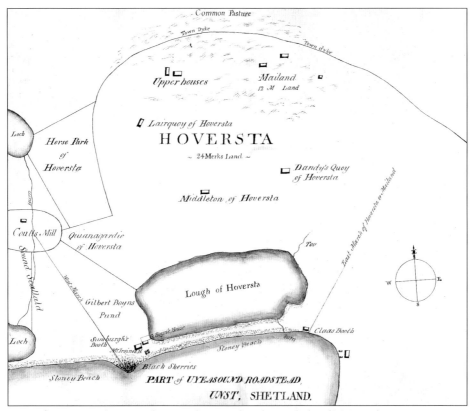

Map of Uyeasound, Unst, showing houses, booths and the divisions between property, annotated "sketch of Hoversta explanatory of the case between Mr Mouat and Mr and Mrs Irvine, 1816".

The severe fever Anno 1736, great scarcity begun Anno 1737 and ended not before 1743 in which time many people dyed, with the very mortal Small Pox Anno 1740 surely third the habitants; and I think the tenants did not increase before 1749 or thereby."[5] In addition agriculture itself was primitive; subsistence living left small margins and many animals died every winter from hunger.

Fish was the mainstay of the Shetland economy. Foreign merchants, predominantly German, bought the fish from the fishermen, a process described by Brand in 1700:

> These merchants seek nothing better in exchange for their commodities than to truck with the country for their fishes, which when the fishers engage to, the merchants will give them either money or wares which(ever) they please, and on the fishers going to sea, what they take, they bring them once in the week, or oftener as they have occasion, and lays them down at their booth door... and the merchants accounts for them accordingly.[6]

The merchants who came for ling, cod and skate supplied in return the necessaries of life, fishing gear, meal, beer and spirits, and household items like linen cloth, shoes and soap which Shetland could not produce itself. Their annual appearance at the trading booths they established on the beaches, these arrangements being regulated by the local foud and bringing some rent to the local landowner, was part of life's normal pattern.

Risk was part of life for everyone, which made the stern certainties preached by the church reassuring, and its grip on social and sexual mores acceptable. The parish was the unit of government which touched the people most nearly. Here local justices charged with the maintenance of law and order coexisted – and were often the same persons as – heritors, the local landowners whose duty and obligation it was to maintain the church and the ministry both financially and practically. In 1667 Commissioners of Supply were established in each Scottish parish, initially to raise the annual land tax, the "cess", but, increasingly, as other duties were added to their portfolio, an important element in local government. After 1707 a formal qualification for appointment, property valued at the fairly low level of £100 Scots[7] per annum, was established, confirming the local basis of the system.

The pattern of landholding in Shetland was of scattered and fragmented holdings. The small numbers of relatively wealthy men, almost all of Scots descent, owned land, sometimes quite a lot of land, in small lots widely separated, usually related to family or other social connections. Their income came both from land rents and the produce of their own animals, and sometimes they were involved with trading or fishing ventures. Those who had land tried to increase their holdings; those who prospered in other ways invested in it. Thus John Neven of Lunning, a notary, acquired property in Bressay including, in 1660, the island of Noss to the east of Bressay, from the Copenhagen Company, one of the Scandinavian interests who were by then divesting themselves of their Shetland holdings.

By the time William Henderson moved to Bressay, it was becoming apparent that the familiar trading arrangements with German merchants were faltering. By the 1680s protectionist customs dues were being levied by the British government on foreign merchants; and the difficulties of the German traders were compounded by the effects of overfishing in Shetland inshore waters. The numbers of visiting merchants fell; and continued to fall. War also had a disruptive effect. Shetland, strategically sited athwart the northern European trade routes, was sometimes the target of direct attack – plundering by privateers was not uncommon, and French forces, raiding during the 1690s when England was at war with France, destroyed crops and houses and carried off cattle.[8] In 1703, the French destroyed the Dutch fleet as it lay at anchor in Bressay Sound, putting an end to the Dutch annual visitations, and also ending the trade in woollen stockings, formerly a useful cash income to many families. Individuals faced financial ruin as the aftermath of war and disruption caused the old systems of trade and earning a living to falter and disappear.

It was during these uncertain years that Shetland landowners began to take a more active interest in trade. Some had already gained wider economic experience through trading the rent commodities of the Earldom estates[9] to Scotland when they were let for the first time to local tacksmen during the 1670s. By about 1700, in the absence of the familiar foreign merchants, local landowners turned their attention to the export of fish and in the years after 1712 they came to dominate the business to the virtual exclusion of all others.

Perhaps the decisive step was the scheme initiated in 1709 by the merchant Robert Jolly whereby external merchants would contract to buy and uplift Shetland exports, with the island end being entirely organised by local people. This scheme involved the kind of men whose landholdings were small and were looking for alternative sources of income. The principal movers were Thomas Gifford of Busta, and William Henderson of Gardie. This arrangement was rapidly followed by a move into taking charge of all the other aspects of the export trade, and the involvement of most Shetland landowners with it.

The export trade was a business, and relied critically upon continuity of supply. It is not surprising that the men running it hit upon the idea of agreeing with the fishermen to lease them some land in return for their services as fishermen. With only a small labour force available, the interest of the landlord was to retain his tenants. As tenants men paid rent for their farms in kind – fish oil and butter – and money; and they fished for the landlord as a trading agreement whereby he supplied the necessaries including the boats to enable them to do so. The distinction between the two arrangements inevitably, rapidly, became blurred. But with replacements hard to find, tenants knew their own value. In 1733 some tenants of Magnus Henderson in Bressay, angry at not being "counted with" for several years, threatened to leave their holdings, no doubt wishing to find a better place to work and avoid the fate of some others who had "thereby become insolvent", a direct result of poor management.[10] Some twenty years later, when Magnus Henderson's son James was fighting off bankruptcy, his Edinburgh lawyer wrote in one memorial on his troubled affairs that "Gairdie (i.e. James Henderson) should inform him by first occasion whether the tennants have stopp'd payment to him upon the summons being execute or whether he thinks they will..." which suggests the reaction of tenants to new situations had to be taken into consideration (March 1756).

As time went on the tenant/landlord relationship became, in the nature of human affairs, more complicated. Most estates, just as much as their tenants, became economically dependent on the success of the fishings. But since annual production both in fish and agricultural produce was inevitably varied, the result was that all parties, in effect, lived hand to mouth, unable to plan ahead. In addition, landowners, already in a situation of financial uncertainty, needed to produce an unknown amount of seasonal credit for their tenants. Such a system stretched resources to the limit, especially in bad years. It was not helped by Shetland's chronic lack of an adequate money supply. The end of the

Dutch trade early in the 18th century removed the main source of cash to ordinary people; but even merchants could find themselves literally without money in the house. Thus in 1756 William Spence, merchant in Yell, had to send to William Mouat, merchant in Uyeasound in Unst, asking him to pay the bearer twenty shillings, "I happening not to be in cash". The extent to which Shetland was a non-money economy lay at the root of many difficulties; without cash, that essential oil for the wheels of commerce, economic life could not develop.

William Henderson, however, found that his move to Bressay had been well worthwhile. When his father-in-law died, he carried on alone; he was called "Skipper" himself now. His later career shows that he acted as one of the prime movers in Shetland economic development, doubtless on close terms with Gifford of Busta. Henderson was successful, or rather perhaps, he was not bankrupted by any catastrophic storm or act of piracy. But although William Henderson's trade was a high-risk venture, he himself was far from flamboyant. Any money he made he invested in land. When, in 1700, he wrote a disposition of land at Petafirth in Bressay, his house at "kelbester banks" was full of small children – five-year-old Magnus and his younger siblings, Charles, Margaret and Elizabeth. That same year Henderson acquired the island of Noss from John Neven, and although he bought bits and pieces of land – in Whalsay, Unst, North Yell – it was Bressay which most interested him. His aim was clearly to own the whole island.

After the death of his first wife William Henderson remarried. Katherine, the widowed youngest daughter of the large family of John Mitchell of Berrie, bore him two more children, another son, William, and a daughter, Jean. Their father's years of effort, of scrimping and saving – an attitude of mind which became ingrained – meant some security, but they would not be idle; the Presbyterian work ethic held Gardie in thrall, and he expected no less of his children. Education was essential, even if he winced at the cost. Indeed, his Edinburgh agent, Charles Mitchell of Uresland,[11] had to rebuke him in May 1718 for "scrupling to send up your son Charles to the College upon any such pretence as you write... lose no opportunity of sending him up for his timeous education." Charles did indeed go to Edinburgh, where the delights of life seem to have led him astray, if temporarily. He never returned to Shetland; one of the many who quietly vanished from the islands, he became a schoolteacher in Charleston, Carolina. His older brother Magnus, however, heir to the

Signatures of members of the Henderson family, collected and annotated by Thomas Mouat (1748-1819), "when idle and fit for nothing better".

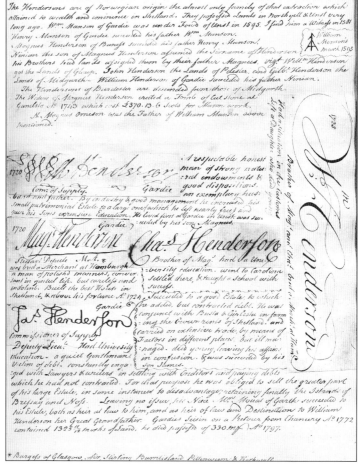

growing Henderson wealth, was educated at Aberdeen University and then sent to learn the family business in Hamburg, the great north German port which at that time was the centre of the Shetland fishing trade.

Magnus Henderson gave every indication of fulfilling the hopes of his father. Clever and quick-witted, he rapidly acquired the "polished manners"[12] which contributed to the favourable impression he made on first acquaintance. He began to acquire the essential contacts in the Scots mercantile world which eventually secured him the office of Burgess in a string of trading towns, business friends to ease his path in Hamburg. It may be conjectured that he also impressed my Lord Morton,

Chamberlain of Shetland, whose residence was at Aberdour in Fife. Henderson, when in the locality, would most certainly have called to pay his respects to this important man. It is quite possible that there, through Morton's good offices, he visited the nearby house of Kinross, the crowning achievement of Morton's late close friend, Sir William Bruce. Here Magnus Henderson was touching the fringe of high society. Bruce (c. 1630-1710) had played some unspecified role in the Restoration of Charles II in 1660, for which he was richly rewarded for much of his life, holding among other offices the post of Surveyor General of the King's Works from 1671-78. Besides his political career he had a considerable reputation as an architect, advising various relatives and noblemen on the rebuilding of their country houses. His own house at Kinross in Fife (built 1679-1690) stands testimony to his genius. It illustrates too how the gentry were beginning to want lighter and more comfortable houses now that defence was not a primary consideration. These lessons, of the new men living in a civilised manner with wider interests than the demands of stark necessity, perhaps suggested to the young Shetlander, for the first time in his life, that new horizons could mean more than the literal phrase.

In 1717 Magnus was recalled from Hamburg by his father:

> ... since I find myself upon the declining hand as to my personal health, and ... this swelling at my breast increasing which I believe will shorten my time here ... if ye could consult a good Doctor of Physick and get some good recept to purge my stomach [you] may do it,

wrote Gardie; adding, prudently:

> if my God hath any more use for me here I shall not neglect the means of promoting life.

He missed his son:

> ...let [God] do with me as he pleases I am content, only desires your company and rests your affectionate father...

Magnus dutifully came home; thenceforth, though his travels were far from over, he was based in Shetland. There his father oversaw his initiation into the home end of the family business. By 1721 Gardie gave up trading entirely, handing over his goods and lands to Magnus, and arranging matters with his usual prudence so as to preclude "any debates and questions that may arise after my death" between his three sons.

The advent of a young, energetic and self-confident personality on the Shetland scene elicited the response which it often engenders to this day – a rapid involvement in many facets of island life (usually followed sooner or later by disillusion on both sides). Magnus Henderson took over the family business, capitalising on his father's personal and commercial ties with the leaders of Shetland enterprise and, evidently, readily accepted by them as a partner in their business affairs. In 1721, aged 26, he formed an association with Gifford of Busta (and with others too at times, notably Nicholson of Lochend and Mitchell of Girlsta) to take a tack (lease) of the Lordship estate. The intention was to develop trade, since the rents produced in kind – butter and oil – would be traded, usually to Leith. Magnus also set up different trading agreements with other contemporaries. That same year he contracted with George Pitcairn of Muness to trade within the whole south parish of Unst and the island of Fetlar, with local agents to act for them, the fish to be divided equally and each to export his own share. Henderson also acted for other landowners who were not directly engaged in trade. In 1727 he exported the fish and oil delivered to him at Bressay by Hector Scott of Scottshall.

Most significantly Magnus Henderson continued the family association with Busta which had started with his father. It was normal eighteenth century practice to underpin the fabric of political and commercial life by the bestowal of offices and other benefits on allies and supporters. In Shetland this probably explains his appointment as Steuart (ie Sheriff) Depute and Admiral Depute of Shetland. These public offices were not sinecures – the Steuart Depute was responsible "for administering of justice to the lieges and punishing of malefactors, conform to the laws of Scotland"[13], and the post of Admiral Depute was potentially highly lucrative, carrying as it did rights of Admiralty in the proceeds of wreck and the stranding of whales, both fortuitous assets and eagerly sought after.

Magnus Henderson left few letters and none of a personal nature, so he must be judged by his actions and by the reactions of others to him. Gifford of Busta evidently regarded him as an ally. "I am resolved to stand by and suport your intrest as far as I am capable," he wrote in a letter of

November 1719, "... so long as we stick together may be very eassy about the efforts of many designing our hurt in this place but in case of spliteing might afford a notable handle to the malicious."

Magnus Henderson was a generation younger than the powerful men to whose counsels he was now privy. Such expressions of confidence suggest that he presented well. What lay behind the self-confident façade only time would tell.

His father seems to have approved of him. The old man was much harder on his youngest son William, now in his turn working in Hamburg and kept on a very tight financial rein. In vain did William point out to his father that a certain style of living was essential to successful business "although I cannot desire extravagances yet unless I be neighbour like can never expect to be looked on here". Nor did the ageing Gardie pay any heed to the young man's plea to be allowed to travel.

> "I should be glad if convenience could allow to see the world like our friend Mr Innes who is gone to travel through the eastern countries, and on his return is to go for Holland, to manage business for his uncle ..."

Logic and emotion were alike ignored. William's yearning for wider horizons was denied him; dissatisfaction with his lot set in early and seems to have coloured a short and not altogether happy life ("my

Shipping in Bressay Sound.   © *Shetland Museum*

misfortune was to be brought up abroad in the merchantile way which requires little more writes than Debt and credit", he commented in 1742).

Meantime as his brilliant elder brother cut a high profile swathe through Shetland society, acquiring in the process the title "young Gardie", the personality traits of their father William Henderson hardened as he aged and, as often happens, laid up trouble for the future. In 1722 a dispute erupted between old Gardie and Arthur Nicolson of Lochend, over monies due to Lochend at the winding up of their joint trading company. There was no dubiety about it – Gardie's refusal to pay stemmed simply from stinginess – and Lochend was naturally extremely angry. But the two had known each other a long time, they were brothers-in-law and had hitherto been on excellent terms ("I stand in company with you on everie matter as formerly," William had written to him in 1717, "wishing the Almighty to direct you in all your undertakings, and that we may have a heartsome meeting..."). Lochend therefore attempted to settle the matter amicably, through the good offices of an arbiter. However, neither Girlsta nor Busta was willing to undertake that difficult task, which left Lochend with no alternative than legal proceedings. This meant a journey to Edinburgh. However, Lochend died suddenly "before the ship he proposed to take his passage by returned from Hamburg" . His demise did not solve the problem; it merely left it in abeyance. Magnus Henderson's part in the affair, if any, is unknown; but he must have known about it. The question is, did he understand the potential for trouble, and did he try to persuade his father to settle. Or, most damningly, did he just do nothing.

Perhaps at this time Magnus Henderson was simply preoccupied. He was contemplating marriage. His bride was to be Elizabeth, daughter of his associate James Mitchell of Girlsta. She had all the necessary attributes for a Henderson bride: young, healthy (and therefore likely to produce healthy babies) and appropriately connected. (The hard-headed side of marriage alliances did not preclude softer feelings. The words of Barbara Montgomerie, pining for her husband Robert Sinclair during the summer of 1716, speak of parted lovers in any age:

> My dier, this has been a lonely summer to me many ways. All your business is now in agitation ... I give my love and blising to you my dir Robe and to my two bernies ... the Almight God send us a quick and comfortable miting which is the earnost desayer of, my dir, your loving and affectionat wife. (3 July 1716.)

Whatever the feelings between Magnus and Elizabeth, it was the decision to marry which precipitated the most long-lasting act of Magnus Henderson's life – the building of Gardie House. By this time it was customary in Shetland for gentry or prosperous merchants to build haas. Originally these were two-storey, thick-walled houses with irregular smallish windows, although they later became more regular in form, and haa houses of differing sizes continued to be built well into the 1800s.[14] Many are lived in to this day.

Magnus Henderson did not want a haa. He wanted one of the new, fashionable, graceful country houses now being built in Scotland, designed by the Scots architects Sir William Bruce and James Smith, and now increasingly popular for very good reasons – handsome in appearance, comfortable within. A frequent plan was of a piendroofed box with the main apartments on ground and first floor, with smaller rooms to the sides and rear. This innovative design took account of the beginnings of consumer demand for houses that were lighter to live in and easier to clean than the grim old buildings they superceded. To build such a house anywhere was to proclaim yourself one of the new generation; in Shetland it must have been extraordinary. It is easy to imagine the wagging of censorious heads as the building began to arise at its site on the green banks of Keldabister in the spring of 1724.

Magnus Henderson's new house had 3ft thick external walls and an internal H-shaped stiffening of 4ft walls. The hundreds of tons of stone required were shipped round to the site from the quarries at Aith in the north of Bressay under the direction of Magnus's Aberdeenshire masons. His account of the expense involved gives details of payments to the skilled men who undertook it – £388 Scots to Thomas Morton, mason, and £112-16/- to John Forbes; £369-15/- for the wages of "quarryers, boaters and workmen"; costings of the materials required, wood, stone, lime, glass and white lead; finally "oak for my windows and door" £162. The total came to £5701-8-4d, Scots money (£475 –2-4d sterling).

As it took shape the building achieved solidity without heaviness, with beautifully proportioned rooms. Some were very large: the two main apartments, one on the ground floor and one immediately above it on the first floor, measure 20' by 30', an astonishing size when one considers the average size of Shetland houses at the time. The building, facing just south of west, enjoys sunshine (when it appears) for all the

An artist's impression of the building of Gardie House in 1724. © *Mike Finnie*

daylight hours, and the rooms are classically proportioned. The first floor drawing room, with its five windows facing the sea, has been described as "one of the half dozen most beautiful rooms in Scotland."[15]

Like all large houses, Gardie House became the hub of a cluster of buildings, which provided the necessary service facilities. These included a mill on the nearby burn, a byre, a dairy, and a garden, situated to the north-east of the house. No record exists of the plan of the garden, but Gifford's nearly contemporary description of "gentlemen's small gardens" suggests vegetable growing: "very good roots, such as turnips and parsnips" he wrote, "also gooseberries, currants, strawberries and artichokes", and maybe even "the herbs and flowers as grow in the north of Scotland, if pains be taken about them."[16] Magnus Henderson would have seen such productive gardens on his travels; it is probable that he wanted one for himself; probable too that this was yet another task for his wife to undertake. Betty had much to do, running her large new house, something not made easier by the fact that it was internally unfinished; making sure it functioned as home and suitable backdrop for her husband's busy life, and producing babies at regular (rather frequent) intervals.

Magnus Henderson's account, in his own handwriting, of expenses incurred in the building of Gardie House , 1724.

Gardie House incorporated the new ideas about domestic buildings. It had big rooms, chimneys, stone slate roof, stone and wooden floors. There were no wall beds, in itself a sign of modernity, since four-poster beds were still a novelty in Scotland. The ground floor was floored with stone flags, and a bread oven with its own chimney was built beside the great fireplace. This was a communal space.

The family's personal apartments were on the floor above, reached by three staircases; and one of these, a circular stone spiral, reached as far as the top of the house, a great empty space beneath the roof, useful for storage but otherwise unused. There is no inventory of the house contents from that date, but merchants' wives would have had the pick of what came home in the ships' holds, and it can be assumed that Betty was no different. At about the same time Nicolson of Lochend, Gardie's brother-in-law, had in his house in Lerwick "a bed in the south room hung with blue camblet (linen) with yellow galoons (ornamental ribbons)" and "a bed in the study hung with blue and white damask" as well as stools "covered with yellow cotton satin". When it could be afforded, Shetlanders liked colour and comfort as well as anyone else, and they, like their Scots contemporaries, began to want items like linen, blankets, coffee, sugar, tea. As yet the prerequisite of the few, they did not remain so: tea drinking in Shetland quickly became generally popular, and indeed a staple.

It is to be hoped that Magnus Henderson was pleased with his house, for it overstretched him financially. His complex business empire was run through intermediaries, factors, who worked for him. This system only works if the owner keeps a close eye on proceedings. But Magnus was to be categorised as "*careless and indolent*"[17] by a later, astute, observer. It is true that the second generation which has not known the struggle of the first is often less stringent in attitude.

He certainly could be lax in business dealings. As early as 1717 Charles Mitchell of Uresland, the Hendersons' agent in Edinburgh, had complained to William Henderson that "your son has not remitted me one farthing as yet albeit in your letter you assured me of considerable remittance again this term". Years later Magnus Henderson's father-in-law, James Mitchell of Girlsta, in Edinburgh on business during the summer of 1732 (he hated it: "I ... resolve patiently to await the conclusion of my affairs at this place and take farewell of it never to return any more if once at home in safety") wrote to warn Magnus Henderson that his agent David Anderson, whom Girlsta thought "truly ... to be ... carefull and active in your business" was so exasperated by Henderson's failure to return "one of the two copies of the signed account he sent you by your sister, notwithstanding he wrote you very pressingly to send him your one signed by you ..." that until he did so

The old byre at Gardie House. Built at the same time as the main house, it contained a dairy, a henhouse, and other service accommodation including a two-seater lavatory which drained into the midden.

Anderson "means not to meddle with what hereafter you may recommend to his care".

To some extent Magnus Henderson could bluff his way through; he was now "a person of considerable address and influence" and "often overmatched those who came up against him"[18] but this was not a solution to the underlying problem; bullying never is. Debts began to accumulate – no uncommon situation this, in an age where entanglements of debit and credit were often entered into as a way out of immediate difficulties and estates normally existed on a financial structure of debt and mortgage. The problem was that such situations had a nasty habit of becoming virtually unresolvable. In 1729 Magnus travelled to Hamburg to resolve a dispute over debts owed to Robert Barclay "anent purchasing of Zetland fish", but no money was paid – the debt was merely transferred to one of the Lerwick merchants, William Bruce.

In particular Gardie was troubled by the repercussions of two situations. The first derived from dealings over the Muness estate in Unst. The Muness lands, formerly owned by the dangerous and overbearing Bruce of Cultmalindie who presided over the North Isles of Shetland from his strategically sited castle of the same name, had fallen on bad times. Various sharp eyes glimpsed potential gains. It was later alleged[19] that in 1719 Magnus Henderson, in concert with Busta, Girlsta and Charles Mitchell, had formed an unholy alliance to pick off the best of the Muness lands. Their instrument was the adventurer George Pitcairn whose marriage to one of the Bruce girls, "whom he used barbarously"[20] enabled him to get his hands on the estate. Meanwhile the true heir, Gilbert Bruce of Clivocast, "having no male heirs and being an old man was tampered with, and induced by the most sinister means to give up the tailzie [entail]." This story of greed and power did no good to those who perpetrated it, as things turned out (though in passing the beauty of the legal phraseology may be noted: "... with the haill houses biggings yards tofts crops tummocks quoys queylands outbrecks outsets annexes connexes meadows mosses muirs pastures grassings parts pendicles and haill righteous pertinents and privileges thereto belonging ..." Extract from a disposition granted by George Pitcairn of Muness, 1719.)

In 1727, whilst the ramifications of these dealings were far from resolved, Magnus Henderson entered into an agreement with Patrick Pitcairn of Dreghorn over debts due on the Quendal estate and he did so without taking the advice of his Edinburgh agent David Anderson. This was a bad move; he very soon regretted it and he was right to do so, for the sum due began mercilessly to accumulate. Tensions increased. George Pitcairn was frightened, his affairs becoming increasingly desperate. "God knows I would doe anything," he wrote to Gardie, "to see you relieved and myself easie." In January 1732 there was a nasty encounter described by Pitcairn: "... after I had bade farewell to you and your brother ... your brother [came] into the room where I was and all at once surprise me with a personal attack and with him such persons as he have trusted ... I was seized behind my back and between with abuses by them ..." Even so, in dealing with Gardie, Pitcairn did not dare to finish the letter with other than protestations of good will and friendship; and in fact he left Shetland the next year and it was said that he died miserably in America, perhaps an instance of wishful thinking.

Following the death of his father in 1728 which deprived him of the old man's advice, Magnus Henderson became increasingly enmeshed in lawsuits. One was with his former associate Charles Mitchell. In 1730 Scott of Scottshall had a case against him as far as the Court of Session. In addition John Nicolson of Lochend had every intention of pursuing him for the unresolved matter of the 1717 debt owed his late brother, litigation only avoided by Nicolson's own death in 1731 when Magnus Henderson promptly had himself appointed Tutor (guardian) to Lochend's children – his own niece and nephew – thus eliminating for the present the possibility of legal action.

But not all Magnus Henderson's actions were confrontational. Nearer to home there are illustrations of the extent to which a local bigwig could act as banker for his community. In the spring of 1732 Magnus Henderson agreed with the minister of Bressay, John Duncan, measures to expedite the building of a new manse.[21] This was of course to be financed by the heritors, and the matter was in Edinburgh where sundry legalities fell to be settled. As the case took its leisurely course through the lawyers' hands, Duncan, understandably keen that building work should begin – he having been, in a deliciously telling phrase, "destitute of a manse" for several years – agreed with Magnus Henderson how this should be achieved. Henderson was to supply the wood, glass, and other essential materials "at easy rates" and to pay the masons, wrights and slaters, while Duncan undertook to ensure that the stone needed was safely on site for the work to begin without delay. He was to pay the other tradesmen, the "quarries, barrowmen and all hired servers of the workmen", and feed them (with assistance from Gardie if required) during the time of the building. Last but not least he was to keep careful records so that once Edinburgh had pronounced, individual financial liabilities could be calculated.

That this arrangement worked successfully is perhaps suggested by the fact that the following year Magnus Henderson entered into another local agreement, this time with the Bressay schoolmaster Walter Robertson.[22] This was a three year contract – it ran from the preceeding Whitsunday – whereby the children who attended the public school in Bressay were to be given free tuition in English, the principles of religion, and the ordinary Church tunes (such a proviso nowadays would greatly benefit hymn singing at Shetland funerals). Lessons in Latin and Arithmetic were to be paid for quarterly "for the same as their parents or

Concerns and he can agree". Mr Robertson was also to "serve the Laird of Gairdie (sic) as his Chaplain, and to be at his call to serve him in every thing that's agreeable to his station and at all times when he is not obliged to attend the School hours..." For this his annual salary was to be one hundred merks Scots money, paid by Magnus Henderson or his heirs and successors, who, in addition, undertook to maintain Mr Robertson and his family in "Bed, board, washing, coal, candle and in every thing proper and necessary to one in his station."

This agreement, however, was at least in part of short duration. In October that same year (1733), Gardie himself died at the early age of 38. The cause of his death is unknown. It was certainly a catastrophe for his wife and children, the youngest a year old baby. His unhappy widow now faced, not only the multiple uncertainties of any woman in her predicament, but the long drawn out retribution of the vengeful.

NOTES:

1   Court Book of Orkney and Shetland, 1625.
2   *History of the Bressay Church*, Stella Sutherland.
3   Thomas Mouat of Garth, Annotated Signatures, 1814.
4   Laurence Bruce of Cultmalindie came to Shetland in 1571; his behaviour was such as to provoke a complaint to the Privy Council in Edinburgh, following which he was disciplined; an inveterate enemy to his uncle Earl Patrick Stewart, executed in 1615. Cultmalindie built Muness Castle in Unst in 1598, and died in 1617.
5   GHA 1782/838.
6   J. Brand *A brief description of Orkney, Zetland, Pightland-firth and Caithness* p17.
7   Scots money differed in value from English – by 1603 the Scots pound was equal to one-tenth of a pound sterling. Monetary values are usually identified as either Scots or sterling, the former being worth considerably less.
8   Frances Shaw: *The Northern & Wester Islands of Scotland, their economy & society in the seventeenth century*, Tom Donald, 1980, p 195.
9   Earldom or Lordship estates - crown estates in Shetland, held from 1643 onwards by the Earls of Morton, & sold in 1766 to Sir Laurence Dundas of Kelse.
10 SA 53/2/190
11 Charles Mitchell of Uresland, brother-in-law to William Henderson, became a writer in Edinburgh, acquired an estate in Fife through his second marriage, died 1726.
12 Thomas Mouat of Garth, Annotated Signatures, 1814.
13 Thomas Gifford of Busta, *An Historical Description of the Zetland Islands*, 1733.
14 Michael Finnie, *Shetland, an Architectural Guide*, 1990.
15 Sir John Betjeman to Mrs Margaret Cameron, pers com, 1960.
16 Thomas Gifford, *An Historical Description of the Zetland Islands*, 1733.
17 Thomas Mouat Annotated Signatures, 1814.
18 GHA, 1771/551.
19 Ibid.
20 Thomas Mouat, Annotated Signatures.
21 Gardie House Deeds, 3 May 1732.
22 Gardie House Deeds, 27 August 1733.

CHAPTER TWO

JAMES HENDERSON

... the Presbytery advised the Session of Brassay to persist in their former conduct ... and they think Gardie's claims, unless supported by much more authentick evidence than has yet appeared, ought to be dismissed as obsolete, frivolous and unfounded ....
Extract, Minutes of the Presbytery of Zetland, 14 March, 1775.

When Arthur Nicolson of Lochend died in 1725 his obsequies lasted from the day of his passing – 19th March – until the actual interment on 30th March. The family took care, accordingly, to provide generous amounts of food and drink for all who came, many local people and some evidently from as far as Unst, since John Corner had been despatched north with letters. The funeral costs included a whole cask of brandy, a barrel of white wine, staggering amounts of ale, as well as gin, tobacco, 36 bottles of claret and 3 dozen pipes. As for food, John Tait of Wadbister provided a pig costing £1-4/-, delivered to Lerwick for a fee of 6/-. Flour, meal, and half a cow supplemented the ambulant pork. Lochend's household, of course, went into mourning. The cloth required was dyed black by Francis Heddell and made up by David McKenlay so that family members, children, close relatives, servants and William Henderson the prentice were all suitably attired and shod. The total bill, including £1-4/- to "the officer for making the grave", came to just under £370.

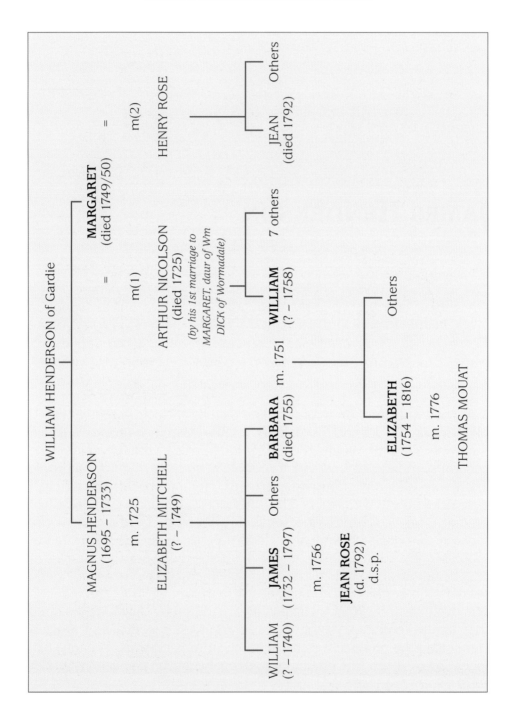

Acco of what was Spent at the Deceast Lochends Funeralls from the 19th March that he departed this life to the 30th Do of his Interrment 1725.

	£	s	d
To Gardy pr particular signd Acco for severall necessaries to the Buriall	69	2	—
To Do Gardy for a Cask of Brandie conform to his Receipt	30	—	—
To William Shearer for 42 pints of Ale @ 3 pr Gardys Acco			
To James Kelday for a 42 pint Cask of ale @ 2	4	0	—
To Andr Bult for 12 Bottles whyt wine	4	0	—
To Jacob Frasser for 2 Casks containing 50 pints @ 3/	7	10	—
To Andr Gifford for a Barrel whyt wine			
To John Moubray for 3 Quarter Casks of ale @ 3/	9	10	—
To William Henderson for one Anker of watters	12	—	—
To cash to John Corner for Expences to Unst in & Letters from Do Henderson	1	10	—
To Do from Do to the Officer for making the Grave	1	4	—
To 14½ Yds of Linnen from John Willson @ 36/ pr Yd	26	2	—
To John Tail in Weddister for one Swine	1	4	—
To James Craigie for 2 Ancors of whyt wine	26	—	—
To cash to a Man for bringing the Swine from Do Tail to Lerwick	—	6	—
To Wormodale for Three Doz of Pipes	—	6	—
To Sumburgh for 36 Bottles of Claret wine	20	—	—
To cash to them for bringing the above bottles of wine from the Ness	2	—	—
To 39 pints of watters from Do: Thomson pd by Gardy & pd by Mr Rose to Gardy	24	—	—
To cash payed by Gardy to them that brought the fores Do 39 pints of watters from Do Thomson & pd P Gardy by Do Mr Rose	—	12	—
To 3 tds wt of Cutt Tobacco from Do	1	16	—
To 3 Doz: fine Pypes from Do	—	16	—
To ¼ pt of a Cow from John Anderson	1	10	—
To cash for the Mort-Cloath & bringing over	3	6	—
To Mr Craigie for 2 lisponds of Flower	6	—	—
To Brackafield for 12 lisponds of Meall @ 24/	14	0	—
To Christian Greig for 4 lisponds of Do @ 24/	4	16	—
To Francis Heddell Dyer for Dying Blacks to the House and Servants conform to his particular signd Acco	31	14	6
To David Mckenlay Taylor pr his Acco	12	0	—
To Harry Irven Shoemaker pr his Acco	12	16	—
To Mournings for Mrs Rose 5 Children, Mrs Taylor, Mrs Jock, Jean Nicolson, Helen Brock, Willm Henderson Printice and Arthur Greig Servant	22	6	—
To John Bourtmaster pr Acco			
To Patrick Laughtine Smith pr his Acco	6	—	—
To Wormodale pr particular Acco	11	—	6

The account of funeral expenses for Arthur Nicolson of Lochend, 1725, showing the food, drink, and other commodities provided for those who attended.

It seems likely that this copious hospitality would also have been provided at Magnus Henderson's funeral in 1732. If it was, some of the bills probably remained unpaid for a considerable while for it quickly became clear that Magnus Henderson had left his affairs in confusion and creditors, no longer deterred by his presence, were becoming increasingly menacing. In addition his Bressay tenants, exasperated by poor management, were demanding that their affairs were sorted out,[1] and, potentially most dangerous of all, a clutch of lawsuits was pending in Edinburgh.

In this situation Magnus Henderson's widow, Elizabeth Mitchell, struggled to cope. Even her marriage contract, which should have safeguarded her own position and that of her children, was found to be "very indistinctly formed".[2] She was assisted by her father, James Mitchell of Girlsta, but he himself was ageing, his own affairs falling into confusion. It is perhaps not surprising that David Anderson, their agent in Edinburgh, found them impossible clients. Elizabeth herself had to be pushed and cajoled into signing such vital documents as the commission which protected her own liferent from the depredations of Magnus Henderson's many creditors. In vain too were the generous efforts of the young William Nicolson of Lochend, who had real grievances against the Hendersons, to come to an amicable resolution; for whatever reason his overtures were ignored, a folly which cost the Hendersons dear.

The story of those years is a litany of general and personal insecurity. Famine came again to the islands between 1739 and 1742, a time known in Orkney as "the years of the short corn". In 1739 the "year's rent or proceeds of the estate [were] ... unfortunately lost by sea"[3]; the following year Elizabeth's elder son William died, probably killed by the smallpox epidemic which carried off so many that year. Her father died in 1742 and in 1743 his estate was declared bankrupt and sequestrated. That same year, however, Elizabeth found the means to spend £370.13.6 on a tomb of cut stone erected in the ancient kirkyard at Gunnista in Bressay for her late husband and her son. Meanwhile William Nicolson of Lochend, who had offered a settlement of his dispute with the Hendersons, sought legal redress in Edinburgh, as did the creditors of the Muness quarrel. In both cases the Hendersons were found liable. The Muness adjudication, being the first and preferential debt, seemed likely to "carry off the entire estate" leaving Elizabeth Mitchell and her children "in utmost hazard of being evicted".[4]

The Henderson mausoleum at Gunnister, Bressay.

When the Nicolson affair came to court, the young James Henderson was held liable for his father's debts, and all his remaining lands went to William Nicolson in payment. Only Bressay and Noss and Gardie House itself remained after, at the eleventh hour, the Hendersons managed to get an old debt due to them repaid. James still had a roof over his head, but the lands so carefully accumulated by his grandfather were gone. His mother died the following year, 1749.

James Henderson grew up in an atmosphere of prolonged uncertainty and with the adults in his life anxious and troubled, not good for any child but not uncommon either. As he matured it became obvious that the new Gardie was not the man his father or his grandfather had been. The drive and ambition which had characterised previous generations were lacking. Most crippling of all, however, was James Henderson's lack of business acumen. His fellows knew it, commented upon it ("had this Gairdie been a man that understood business he never would have behaved as heir..." wrote Arthur Nicolson in October 1763, explaining to his fellow merchant Robert Barclay why pursuing the monies owed him by Gardie would be pointless. "... if his estate was sequestrate at this day, it would not near pay the real debts affecting it ...") and took advantage of it. Gardie floundered in a sea of debt, assailed by paperwork and lacking the ability to tackle his situation.

Nicolson's assessment is borne out by James Henderson's correspondence. He lost letters (or had them stolen, as when in 1762 the *Margaret* of Leith, on her way south with James Henderson's instructions to his Edinburgh agent on board, was carried off to Dunkirk by a French privateer), forgot details – "I have unluckily mislaid [your letter] and do not exactly remember the contents so that I cannot give answer as I ought" – was unable to cope with his more obdurate creditors – "I cannot bring Greenwall to transact with me for that Bond of his ..." and generally made heavy weather of any transaction. His confusion of mind shows in a letter of February 1760 to his Edinburgh agent:

> ... so soon as you receive the money from him you'll pay in £20 of it to Mr John Black and take his receipt for it, in part payment of my Bill to him, which I am sorry should have been so long owing, ... and the remainder with what you have in your hands and the letters of credit I have sent you by this occasion will pay Mr Barclay in case he can be prevailed on to accept of the £300 with interest and expenses, and should he not I must submit to what terms he'll give me and must trust to your procuring the best for me you can ...

He was clumsy in business and in dealing with others and he was not respected, as appears from the comments of various exasperated correspondents. Thus William Spence, merchant in Midyell, wrote in the autumn of 1756:

> "... I shall pass over the accusation of incivility as methinks it's wrong applied, if Gardie can as well reconcile with honour and generosity the promises made more than once to me, when in the North Isles, compared to the late transaction with Mr Robertson of Gossabro, I have only to leave to his own reflection."

Spence responded firmly to what he regarded as an unnecessary reminder of forthcoming rent due to Henderson:

> ... touching the affair of tack duty, I required no remembrance thereof, being resolved to order same at candlemass term, as stipulated by contract. And lest I am then tardy, must submit to the forfeiture.

Others were even more forthright:

> I have only as yet had time to take a very cursory glance at your memorial ... only I can observe that your clerk has misunderstood the meaning of the word 'fact' or pays little regard to it, as I never saw it so often abused in so few pages ...

commented Basil Scott of Voesgarth, Unst, some twenty years later. Evidently Henderson failed to learn from experience.

Where he could, however, James Henderson tried to remain on good terms, even – or especially – when he owed money. A tone of anxious friendliness is evident in his dealings with another merchant, William Mouat[5] of Uyeasound, to whom he owed money:

> I had a letter by Mr Sanderson from your neighbour John Hoseason in Murister wanting a liferent tack[6] to him and his wife, but as I promised to you I do not incline to set that or any other lands in your neighbourhood without acquainting you, so if it be agreeable to you I shall give Mr Hoseason and his wife a tack of the lands. My terms are as follows, that he shall pay two guineas of entry, three lisponds and four merks of butter for butter debt, and fresh ling for the money debt, at 3d each ling. ... I shall have copies [of dispositions] ... made out for you, and have them ready when you come here, so that ... you can have our accounts from last year settled, and when our business is finished, we shall have a crack over a bowl of good rum punch, and don't forget to bring over your son Thomas for a night or two.

William Mouat was much involved in the issues of the day; James Henderson was not. He took no part in public life. He was now the sole survivor of his family; his sister Barbara having died in 1755, leaving two small children by her marriage to Arthur Nicolson of Lochend. Gardie's own marriage, which took place in 1756, was to remain childless. His wife was his cousin Jean Rose, daughter of his redoubtable aunt Margaret[7]. The young couple had their portraits painted to mark the occasion, James earnest in full wig and best coat, Jean simply dressed, fair-haired and wistful.

Jean's little silver cream jug survives, mute testimony to the grander elements of a life which was in many respects to modern eyes exceedingly uncomfortable. They lived at Gardie House, which was cold, dark and damp, with stone floors at ground level and a wooden staircase

James Henderson and his wife Jean Rose. The portraits were probably painted to mark the occasion of their wedding in 1756. Jean Rose was apparently most particular that her clothes should be properly aired – her chemise would be aired overnight under her pillow and then be worn for a day by her niece Catherine Lindsay before Jean would consent to put it on. (Miss Turnbull-Stewart, Lerwick, 1890).

in the centre. Work on the house interior continued slowly when funds permitted. During the 1760s the drawing room was panelled in pine by an itinerant craftsman who also worked at Sir John Mitchell's new haa at Sand (the drawing room panelling there is identical in its detailing).

The 1750s and first years of the 1760s saw good harvests and fishing in Shetland and work for those who wished at the Greenland whaling. The population began to stabilise and to increase, though it was a gradual process. Emigration was always an option. Writing in 1764 William Mouat attributed "the reason of this isle [Unst] not being more populous" to "shipping coming often here, and the youth being generally of spirit, and seeing the sunshine days of the seamen, many go abroad, and ... are rarely ever more heard of, few having ever returned, which indeed is the case of the whole country (i.e. Shetland) in general, though more go from this than any other part." In 1776 a memorial for the fishcurers of Zetland stated that "one hundred men and more for these twenty years back

Detail of the fireplace and wall panelling in the drawing room of Gardie House.

have gone annually from these islands into His Majesty's Navy, and into the other shipping of Great Britain."

Despite this, the islands were beginning to experience their share of the population increase which occurred throughout western Europe during the second half of the 18th century, and whose effects were particularly marked in the Highlands and Islands of Scotland, where the population doubled between 1755 and 1811. Coupled with a run of bad weather and poor fishings, the result was predictable – a crisis of sustainability. The growth of outsets (new arable enclosures) is itself indicative of increasing pressure on land. Significantly, this crisis, which brought endemic food shortages, did not occur in the agriculturally advanced countries of England and Holland.

Robert Barclay, who retired to Edinburgh after a lifetime's trading, lamented the passing of the old ways in a letter to his old friend William Mouat, in 1768. "I cannot be altogether without Zetland ling, I commonly get ½ doz small ones from Leith every winter, which cost me triple price they used to sell for at Hamburg. That trade is I suppose almost if not quite gone now, sic transit gloria mundi."

But some things did not change: in Shetland the uncertainties of subsistence living were compounded by the chronic, crippling shortage of the money supply[8]. The skilled workman Thomas Leslie wrote James Henderson in May 1756, desperate for the contract to supply nails for the repairs to the Bressay kirk. "When I had made about 200 (nails)," he wrote, "I was called to witness the interment of Mr Gifford of Wethersta, and by bad weather was detained at Busta ... I shall without loss of time make 400 more ... I'm not able to purchase any supply at present, and if anything could be spared from your hand it would come very seasonally to a needful family." May was always a bad month, with the winter supplies exhausted and the summer not yet arrived.

James Nicolson of Gloup wrote in April 1766:

> I shall not be surprised to hear that in the present calamitous state of the country in general, the people who have neither to save their ling nor sow their lands do masterfully force from those who have to spare, who certainly should it so happen will have a poor chance of redress nor indeed does anyone desire it that has either so bad a heart or head as hoard uselessly up what his neighbour must starve for want of ... I am also glad for the first time of the Greenlanders [whalers] to appear on our coasts ... I am hopeful they'll relieve some poor people, who tis to be feared might otherwise starve.

Pressure on land brought its own problems and stresses. In Bressay advertisements were posted on the church door exhorting the proper upkeep of fences and dykes. One, in July 1777, concerned the people of Keldabister, who "allowed their sheep to leap over the dykes of Newtown, and find their way to the corn and grass grounds of Cruaster which they have greatly injured and destroyed, to the almost unspeakable loss of the concerned". A year later William Redland had to be compensated for the loss of his oat crop, destroyed by invading sheep from the Ham scattald.

These problems were the province of the landowner; others were the remit of the Church. Bressay kirk session records from 1764 onwards give a picture of everyday life, perhaps not untypical of Shetland in general. Bressay itself formed part of the parish of Bressay, Burra and Quarff, an extraordinarily awkward conjunction of two islands of different sides of Shetland and a landward area approximately between them. The Session met regularly – although meetings might be postponed through bad weather or illness it was not often that this

This watercolour painting by M. A. Cameron, painted in 1882/83, shows Bressay from Lerwick. The kirk can be seen to the left, and the large house on the right is the "new" manse, built in 1819. The old manse, not visible in the picture, still exists.

happened. They met at the Manse, or after a church service. Normally present were the minister, the Moderator (Chairman) of the Session, and the elders, with the Clerk to take the minutes. Their debates and decisions reflect the authority which they held in both the practical and the moral sphere.

Representing as it did the church in its primary interface with its parishioners it is hardly surprising that the Session is best remembered for its stance on sexual morality. Extra-marital sex was strongly frowned on, even if the partners subsequently married; pregnancy was a disgrace. Both these misdeameanors carried the penalty of public censure at church. In November 1765 James Lesk, after at first denying it, acknowledged that he was the father of Grizel Wilson's unborn child, "for which sin and scandal he is appointed to make satisfaction to discipline thru three sabbaths and pay five pound Scots as his penaltie for the poors use". Lesk disliked this prospect so intensely that he disappeared to the island of Fetlar, and it was not until the following November that, following an interview with the minister, and an arrangement come to whereby James Henderson of Gardie " obliged himself to pay to the Treasurer, John Bigg, upon demand, ... James Lesk's fine", that he was "sharply rebuked, before the congregation, and ... reposed to the privileges of the church". No such escape was possible, of course, for the unfortunate girl involved; church services were often attended by one or more women held up to public censure, whether or not the man involved stood by them.

Elders were aware of the "frequent immoralities prevailing in some Towns", and their numbers were reinforced specifically to combat this, as happened in 1770, when Malcolm Halcrow and James Smith in Aith, Malcolm Linklater in Gunnista, and James Duncan in Midgarth were appointed "in order for the more suppressing vice and immorality in this parish". The Session also tried to promote good behaviour: disturbed by George Neilson using "unchristian expressions" against Nicol Halcrow "to the dishonour of God and great hurt of religion", the Session summoned him to be rebuked before the congregation the following Sabbath.

Occasionally situations were not so amenable to community pressure. In October 1768 George Bult of Beosetter made a complaint:

> ... that Magnus Georgeson in Byoster has most scandalously abused him
> by horrid curses and imprecations, viz, he prayed God dam the

Complainer's dogs face, and that repeated times, and if he had been born he the Complainer was whelped, I had been as good as thou, and cursed on for about three hours time ...

At the next meeting of the Session Magnus Georgeson arrived with a written defence, utterly denied the complaint against him, and when "the moderator interrogate the Defender, if he could undertake to prove the particulars in the above paper signed by him? He answered he could prove every one of them." The Session wisely recognised that this affair was beyond their capabilities; they instructed the Clerk to put the whole matter in the hands of Mr Malcolmson, Clerk to the Sheriff Court in Lerwick.

It was difficult to stop breaches of the Sabbath. When in May 1772 an English ship lay in at Cullingsbrough and the local people traded with her that Sunday, they were all duly rebuked after the church service; a more blatant case occurred a year later when William and Alexander Gifford of Pettifirth went off in their boat "when the Congregation was convening for public worship, and notwithstanding they were prohibited to proceed by the minister, in sending his servant to them..." Andrew Anderson of Grindiscol, also implicated, told the Session "the ships to which his boat went off upon the Sabbath day had put out a signal for him, being an acquaintance, and having a sick man on board they wanted his advice to get a Doctor to let blood him, which was a work of necessity, and did not think it a breach of the Sabbath day". Whatever the Session's opinion of this excuse, it could do no more than to insist that unless there were distress signals, they were not to go on board ships on the Sabbath. In vain, one suspects, did the Moderator attempt to appeal to Bressay finer feelings by retailing how he had been asked "by the better sort of people in Lerwick, how his said parishioners presumed to break the Lord's Day ?" (July 1775).

The tenor of complaint and judgement over the years indicate that where individuals stood up to them, albeit circuitously, the Session was sensitive to the limits of its authority. But it was also concerned with practical matters and here its members acted with common sense and humanity. They paid the funeral expenses of the poor. They authorised the buying of improving books to be sold to the people "for the use of familys and children". They had a mortcloth, bequeathed by James Bult of Cruister, available to hire for use at funerals at a cost of 2/- Sterling (though inevitably some complained that one could be got from Lerwick at less cost). They issued testimonials of good behaviour to assist those leaving home, like Marjory Lamb in Brough and Sicly Isbister in Keldabister, bound for London in August 1766, and inspected those of some who returned, like Grizel Smith, wife of William Gifford in Pettifirth, whose testimonial was signed by the Scots minister in Rotterdam.

The Session's most important task, however, at least to modern eyes, was in dealing with the poor of the parish and alleviating distress. It may be noted that their concern extended further than their own small boundaries. At least twice the Session authorised payment to unfortunates who were strangers. In July 1771 the church collection of £4-6/- was given "to supply two men who were hurt by accident of the firing a gun in their ship", and the following year the Minister and elders, in conclave at the manse, granted eighteen pounds Scots money, part of the total from several collections, to "strangers cast in through distress of weather to the Parish of Walls ... who were upon their voyage to North America". Ex gratia payments were made from the Poor Box, like the two guineas to Jean Andrew in Brough to clothe her naked children (March 1775). And when James Yorston presented a funeral account for Margaret Dempster, "a poor young woman he brought to his house through charity, and not as a servant", the Session paid it, or most of it but, wary of the implications, "resolve and agree that if any other head of a family bring such objects from other parishes for the future, without the session's concurrence therein, ... they shall be obliged to maintain and bury such objects ... without any relief from the Session." (1767).

Relief of want was mainly concerned of course with local people. It was the constant concern of the Session to be aware of "the Poor in their Quarters who are indigent and receives no supply from the Session". With a finite amount of money at their disposal, the Session had to be realistic – if a pauper's circumstances changed, he might no longer be helped, like James Smith in Gremista in the summer of 1766, who, after he "received some mony from his friends in Holland to support him, the Session thought proper to drop him at present". Charity was either in cash or in kind. In May 1765:

> ... the Session taking under their serious consideration that the price of victual in this country is like to rise very high this summer, and as their Moderator is going to the parish of Dunrossness to preach there (in their Minister's absence attending the General Assembly of the Church of

Scotland) they judge it proper to give the Moderator mony to procure six lisponds of meal for the poor of this parish use in their indigent case, and to report.

Normally, however, the Session used James Henderson of Gardie as a combined banker and disperser of charity in kind, normally meal. Once the needy had been identified, the Session would reckon up the total of their poor relief, and "appointed the same to be paid by James Henderson of Gardie in meal and money as usual for this quarter, and the Clerk to give Gardie an extract hereof" (1776). These monies would be "placed by Gardie to the Session's account".

They could respond relatively quickly to situations of distress, as they did in May 1771 when:

...the session taking under consideration the necessitous condition of Ann Smith's family in Hogan judged it reasonable to appoint Gardie to supply that family betwixt this and October next with such a quantity of meal as the Moderator and he shall judge needful for them.

Again that August:

... the Session taking under consideration the state of Agnes Smith's family in Hogan orders Gardie to advance her the sum of ten pounds Scots money by degrees as he sees most proper, as a nursing fee [for] one of her twins, from the birth of said children til a twelve month out, and also to give her for behoof of her blind lass in her house the quantity of six lispunds meal for one year by degrees as he sees proper from this date.

This is the first mention of the "blind lass of Hogan", who was supported by the Session until she disappears from the records fifteen years later. The Session seems to have taken real care of her: in 1774 when the elders were directed to enquire "with respect to the clothes and effects belonging to the poor" specific mention was made "particularly to enquire into the state of the blind lass in Hoghen". (sic)

Paupers were normally allocated one to each township – the four recorded in 1766 as receiving cash payments lived in the towns of Kirkabister, the Mail, Midgirth and Gremista – and normally in a family house. But sometimes there were difficulties, perhaps of personality or behaviour. In 1768 a poor woman, Janet More, asked for help as "none would take her into their house". The Session took what money and effects she had "to be kept and expended for her behoof" – which may suggest some waywardness – and directed John and James Yorston and John Bigg to "look into the poor's house at Gremster and to report what sum will be necessary to make an apartment in said house ..." They then employed some men to do the necessary work and "furnish her some peats".

As time went on the numbers of paupers increased and the amounts disbursed shrank. Accounts were reckoned regularly, and Gardie would come down to the meeting to settle up so that all parties saw it done. The Session did have income. Apart from the fines levied on erring parishioners, which went into the Poor Box, there was the rent from church lands, which the Session found most satisfactory to let by public roup (auction). There were also church seats. These were individually owned and paid for, property rights which could be sold or transferred to others with due care and formality, as did William Tomison of Crueton, when in 1766 being in "straitening circumstances" he sold his desk "upon the north side with the west wall at the back thereof" to the Session, who paid him at the rate of half a crown per month. In 1773 William Manson, tenant in Hoversta, transferred his right to a half share in a desk in the kirk "(bounded by a Table seat possessed by and bonded to Gardie and John Smith in Bruntland etc, to the westward, and the desk belonging to Katherine Gray to the eastward) to Andrew Williamson tenant in Ham and his heirs and successors in all time coming ...".

Events were to combine, however, to produce a situation beyond the means of kirk and landlord to answer. Between 1769 and 1784 there was a succession of bad harvests and bad fishings. In 1772 Andrew Heddell commented about Lerwick : "I never saw a greater appearance of want hereabouts in my life ..."

The ability of landowners to supply credit was exhausted; so were the last cash reserves of the tenants, who found themselves bad debtors, with no likelihood of redemption. Severe winters in the early 1780s caused the heavy losses of livestock, cattle in particular, which in turn brought famine conditions in the winter of 1783-84.[9]

In May 1784 the Commissioners of Supply, clergy and heritors of Shetland sent a petition to the king asking for help in a situation described by Andrew Bruce's covering letter:

... many have already died of mere hunger, and it is to be feared many more will. A very great number of the black cattle, horses and sheep are already dead. The crops for these past 4 years have almost totally failed. The deficiency in the quantity of fish formerly caught is considerable. The tenants, farmers and fishermen are ruined and starving. Their masters are not far from ruin. They are really unable longer to supply these poor creatures; their funds cannot answer the demands on them. Oatmeal although to be bought, was there money to pay for it, is at the enormous price of 24p/boll. Small as the arable grounds are, a large proportion lies unlaboured for want of seed ... Universal ruin seems to pervade the whole inhabitants, Absolute famine has been barely staved off by the humane supplies sent hither gratis by government and another well timed supply by Sir Thomas Dundas.

This busy scene shows vessels typical of those which would have frequented Bressay Sound at the time of James Henderson. © *Shetland Museum*

The result was the necessity of Government intervention for the first time in the century. Two ships, the *Montrose* and the *Struan*, were sent with 500 Quarters of barley and 40 tons of biscuit "got ready with all possible despatch". "I have made use of every argument with the captains to impress despatch on their minds," wrote Simon Frazer, who oversaw the operation in London, "by telling them the great want of provisions in which your islands are ..." To expedite matters he had had the forty tons of biscuit baked by two separate bakers, asking "please tell me if the bread proves equally good or which is best".

Entrusted with the task of overseeing distribution were John Bruce of Sumburgh and Robert Hunter of Lunna, and it was Bruce who wrote back to Simon Frazer in early August to confirm the safe arrival of the ships and their cargoes and its ongoing distribution; the bread he was told "by good judges" was "exceeding good" with little difference in quality except that perhaps that marked G was "rather more even baked."

The Commissioners of Supply, on whose behalf Bruce was acting, had directed him to sell at public action the containers and bags in which the supplies had been packed. "You will please therefore advise me in course if or not I shall remit the proceeds of these sales to you for account of Government. I have no right to give a public opinion on this matter," added Bruce, "but it is my private thought that it would not be inconsistent with the sentiments of his Majesty and Parliament that this trifle should be distributed equally as an additional supply amongst the fatherless and widows in each parish ... but this as you shall direct and advise ..."

By now merchants were replacing landowners as the prime movers in trade. Bruce of Sumburgh gave up his fishings in the 1770s – a move which was opposed by his tenants – and Hunter of Lunna abandoned a similar attempt in 1799. James Henderson of Gardie had always let his fishings, first to the energetic Andrew Bruce of Hogan, who with his neighbour Thomas Bolt of Cruister took a leading role in developing the Spanish market for Shetland fish; later to Arthur Nicolson of Lochend. When Gardie did finally take them back into his own hands he employed a factor. He also moved to money rents. The island of Noss was let to James Copland without condition of fishing before 1793, and Laurence Hughson of Bigtown was granted a ten-year tack of Bressay in 1793.

As time went on James, chronically short of funds, continued to stave off financial collapse by ad hoc means. He added to a business letter of January 1771 to his then agent in Edinburgh, James Marshall WS, a request for funds: "... necessity has compelled me to draw on you for ten pound sterling payable at three months sight to the order of Mr Magnus Fea, merchant in Lerwick, in honouring which draft you'll very much oblige me, and may depend on my utmost endeavours to reimburse you very soon ..." How Marshall's heart must have sunk. But it was Marshall who at last regularised James's title to his lands, and sent him the Precept ("which has cost a hellish deal of money") and sasines for James to sign, some forty years after the death of his father.

After his wife died in 1792 James lived alone at Gardie, attended by his servant Janet Peterson. His heir was Elizabeth Nicolson, his niece; in 1775 she had married Thomas Mouat, elder son of that Unst merchant William Mouat who was one of Henderson's principal creditors. It was typical of Gardie, whose life had been spent attempting to deal with complex situations not of his making, to try to create one all of his own. He began to look for an alternative heir.

He found one in the form of his third cousin Gilbert Henderson of Bardister (1757-1841), now a merchant in the boom town of Liverpool. Gilbert was both plausible and acquisitive, and he had the successful

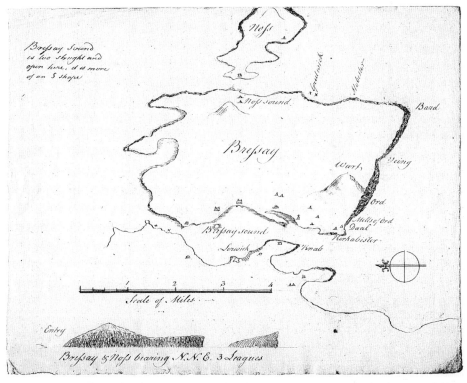

A map of Bressay, Noss and Bressay Sound, showing prominent features, including buildings, obviously intended as a navigational aid. Drawn by Thomas Mouat; undated, between 1790 and 1817.

exile's fondly-coloured feeling for home. The two men explored the possibility of a bargain: in return for Gilbert paying off James's debts, he would be left the whole of Gardie's assets. Elizabeth Mouat, heir by destination, would be paid off with eighty pounds per annum in lieu. Secrecy was essential – James could be in no doubt as to the reaction of the Mouats were they to get wind of the scheme, and he must have known that it was likely to mean litigation. But as he had always done, James saw the immediate staving off of difficulties rather than the longer-term implications. Gilbert came to Shetland on a summer visit in 1796 and went away with a list of groceries and other sundries to be sent to Gardie, ranging from knives and forks to oil of lavender, bergamot, barley sugar, soap and toothbrush and a new set of china; and wood for repairing the house roof.

Gilbert, considerably more worldly wise than his elderly cousin, lost no time on his return to Liverpool in taking legal advice to ensure that the proposed course of action was feasible. Aware of Gardie's ability to procrastinate, he suggested that James should retire to live with them in Liverpool, where no doubt the signing of the bargain could be better accomplished. Various presents were despatched to Shetland – a parrot, a hat and a 20lb Cheshire cheese. James however declared himself unable "to undergo the fatigue of a voyage by sea or journey by land, and therefore must rest satisfied … and spend the few years that may remain of my life in my own country…"

Meantime he sent off to his Edinburgh agent a list of the lands to be disponed to Gilbert. The wood for the house roof was loaded aboard the brig *Ann*. Her delay by contrary winds enabled Gilbert to send a note:

> … of the following interesting details, viz: This day and yesterday the papers announce the receipt of Paris papers of the 20th ult containing the important intelligence of the Emperor of Germany and the French having signed the preliminaries of peace: this was done by the Archduke and Bonaparte in a garden … the Austrians have been beaten on the line and lost 7000 men and 27 pieces of cannon … it is thought that Great Britain is included in the business by the Emperor…[10]

But these world affairs were no longer of interest to James Henderson. By the time the *Ann* dropped anchor in Bressay Sound in August 1797 he was dead, and Gilbert's hopes with him. A fortnight later Thomas and Elizabeth Mouat arrived back in Shetland from a trip to Edinburgh to discover the intended bargain.

NOTES:

1   SA 53/2/190.
2   GHA 1730/305.
3   GHA 1745/334.
4   GHA 1748/338.
5   William Mouat, 1714-1790, merchant at Uyeasound, Unst, later inherited property from his uncle.
6   Tack – lease.
7   Margaret Henderson, sister to Magnus and aunt to James, married Arthur Nicholson of Lochend and after his death married, about 1729, Henry Rose, collector of customs in Lerwick. She was fond of and supportive to her stepson William Nicholson, heir to Lochend, in his dispute with the Hendersons. One of her daughters by her second marriage, Jean, married James Henderson.
8   Hance Smith, Shetland Life and Trade, p 59.
9   Hance Smith, Shetland Life and Trade, p 82.
10   Treaty of Campoformio, concluded October 1797.

CHAPTER THREE

WILLIAM MOUAT

*A silly impulse suddenly struck into Betty Guthrie's head to have
a soldier for her own defences, he is wounded in the arm and blind
of one eye and so they are to be married in a few days, whereby I lose
a willing contented cheerful imperfect but attached fouthie[1] servant
... that is a great loss to me for I know not where to replace it ...*
John Mouat, Annsbrae, Lerwick to William and Eliza Mouat, 1811.

In times of war the voyage between Shetland and the Scottish mainland
held manmade dangers in addition to the familiar hazards of wind and
weather. Fleets of hostile nations were no strangers to northern waters;
during the 1790s when Britain was at war with revolutionary France,
merchant shipping was preyed upon by both the French and the Dutch.
In 1797 the Shetland packet *Duchess of Sutherland* was taken by the
French cutter *Bolognois*, the mail thrown overboard, and the vessel sent
for a prize to Norway.[2] The experience of Thomas and Elizabeth Mouat,
on their way home from Edinburgh earlier that summer, was alarming
enough: a French privateer on the prowl along the east coast of Scotland
chased a vessel ashore at Stonehaven while the Mouats' ship lay in St
Andrews bay; but after a two-day detour into Kirkwall they finally arrived
in Bressay Sound on 23rd August.

There they were met with the news of James Henderson's death. As
always happened, his cabinet and other repositories for documents had
been officially sealed. These were duly opened in the presence of

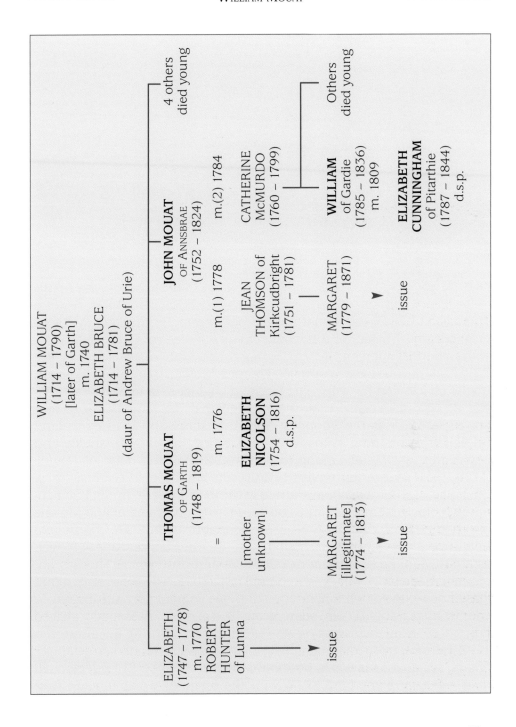

Print depicting ships in Bressay Sound, Fort Charlotte in the foreground, the town of Lerwick clustered on the shore and the Wart of Bressay in the background.

© *Shetland Museum*

Thomas and Elizabeth Mouat as next of kin and Thomas, acting for his wife, became "master of the whole circumstances" of Gardie's dealings with Gilbert Henderson.

If, as events were to prove, Thomas Mouat, then aged 47, could hardly be less like his wife's late uncle in character, in lineage his family was no less respectable than the Hendersons. The Mouats traced their line as far back as the Conquest and their successful journey through Britain brought them lands and royal offices on the Welsh Marches before the first Mouats came to Scotland during the reign of David I (1124-1153). By the fourteenth century the family held two castles, at Buchollie in Aberdeenshire and Freswick in Caithness; in Shetland the name Mouat first appears in a charter of 1572. Of the Shetland Mouats, one branch of the family took its designation from Garth, the original holding above the waters of Sullom Voe. By the 17th century they were established in the North Isles of Yell, Fetlar and Unst, where Thomas, son of a self-made man, was bred to hard work and decisiveness, and to first-hand knowledge of what happened to those without such attributes.

Thomas Mouat had been very ill during the Mouats' visit to Edinburgh. Nonetheless, as he slowly convalesced during the autumn of 1797, he took immediate action to clarify James Henderson's tangled affairs, safeguard his wife's position, and see off Gilbert Henderson. He declined having anything to do with the cargo of wood sent up from

Liverpool, in terms which give a flavour of all the personalities involved: "Gardie would have found many friends whether pretended or real to inform him that Liverpool and all the West of England was the worst mercat in the world to purchase wood at, being generally the best to sell at, and perhaps he was almost the only man in Shetland so unacquainted with business as not to know that." (December 1797).

Thomas Mouat had already turned his attention to James Henderson's long neglected Bressay estate, which was disponed to him by his wife in the summer of 1798. As early as October 1797 he gave instructions to Bressay tacksman Laurence Hughson to convert the archaic services rendered by estate tenants into a money payment, one shilling and sixpence sterling yearly (with, it appears, questionable success, since they still existed some 15 years later)[3]. Hughson was also to collect the house rents from Christian Nicolson and Ann Linklater at the Banks of Keldabister (eight pounds Scots each), and to sell the seats in the kirk which had belonged to Gardie. Four months later Hughson reported the results of sorting out accounts owed and owing, including the sale of the "trifling" number of kirk seats which had belonged to the late Gardie – they were, not surprisingly, "much out of repair".

Others hastened to bring their unpaid bills to Thomas Mouat's notice. Andrew Linklater of Insista, Bressay, in "urgent straits", begged the speedy reimbursement of monies owed him, including his fee for shaving the late Gardie "forty-eight hours after he dyed". Magnus Yorston, who lived at Noss Sound, pointed out courteously but firmly that Mouat's reckoning to him was incorrect. "I was always well used by the late Gardie," he wrote, "and I have every reason from what I have been told of you that I will be no worse used." Mouat responded well to this approach, asking James Linklater in Bressay to settle the account on his behalf, plus any interest due the Yorstons. Mouat, conscious that he knew little of Bressay affairs, consulted the merchant Thomas Bolt, whose family had long owned the lands round their haa at Cruister, a ten-minute walk along the hillside from Gardie House. Bolt knew his history: "I think you will find that Magnus Henderson of Gardie purchased a good many lands in Bressay from Busta ... it was all Neven of Gunnelsta's lands ..." He took a forthright view of the task facing Mouat, who at that point was deep in correspondence with his Edinburgh lawyer. "I will not say that it is unnecessary to consult lawyers sometimes, but I will say that it is seldom I see them give satisfactory answers ... all lawyers have a particular knack of making difficulties more than are necessary..." Bolt commented to Mouat that December, a point of view possibly not without its adherents today.

The island of Noss, viewed from Ander Hill in Bressay.   *Photograph by Jane Manson*

In March 1798 James Copland, tenant of the island of Noss, who had had difficulties the previous year with men building lodges by the north beach or Milns of Noss for summer fishing, wrote to Mouat, alarmed to find that these "villainous pretensions" were evidently to be renewed.

> I therefore think that it is necessary to carry the stones of the lodges to repair the dyke of the enclosure, and as it is some distance to carry these stones and they of a very large size, it will cost some expense and now the labouring season is in, and all my men servants is listed for soldiers with Captain Malcolmson, ... I therefore wish to know if you will desire me to employ men to carry the stones ... my prospect in view at present is but very mean and discouraging and my time here very short ...

Mouat replied that he was perfectly entitled to use the stones as he wished "to improve his farm and upholding his sheep pens", promised to contribute towards the cost, and further reassured him that "until the sheriff's interlocutor was altered no man could molest him about these lodges". Copland's anxiety about his tenancy was unfounded: he held Noss until 1810 and the sheep fanks he repaired, now in their turn becoming ruinous, may be seen slowly tumbling onto the north beach.

As far as Gardie House itself was concerned Mouat thought little of it (his attitude softened later, when he no longer had to pay for its upkeep). Nonetheless, he instantly made arrangements for the roof to be repaired, something James Henderson had been putting off for years if not decades (as long ago as December 1792 Henderson had complained of the effect on his health "by the dampness of having no roof"), and instructed the tacksman[4] Laurence Hughson: "I have 3000 slate lying at Aith which are intended for Gardie's house. I beg you will order the transport of them by your tenants ... and cause them to be carried into the garden and laid up there under John Halcrow's inspection to whom you will give them in charge and then advise me the exact expense."

The house itself was empty. There had been a public roup of the contents in September 1797 as part of Mouat's drive to raise money to clear the Henderson debts, and virtually everything had been sold, including the white gilt china bought in Liverpool that spring by Gilbert Henderson for his cousin James Henderson at a "high" cost of 37 guineas ("but well worth it" Gilbert considered), and all the animals, horses, cattle and sheep.

Mouat's brother John, who lived in Lerwick, suggested that Thomas should come and live at Gardie House. Thomas was having none of it. He had no intention of moving from Unst. And so the house stood for the next decade, empty but kept in repair. A lonelier situation now for Anne Grey, who seemed a permanent fixture in her little house at the end of the garden. She had been servant to Lochend in the old days and housekeeper for the Nicolson children including Thomas Mouat's wife Elizabeth, who supported her financially throughout a lengthy old age. This probably enabled Miss Grey to continue to indulge a partiality for gin and brandy[5]; however, she must finally have died sometime before 1807 when the roof of her house was removed by L. Henry and John McBeath, who spent that summer working on repairs to Gardie House itself and the Bressay schoolhouse.

In 1811 Thomas Mouat's nephew William returned from Edinburgh to live permanently in Shetland. He was now heir to both his uncle and

Oil portrait of William Mouat of Gardie, painted by John Irvine ARSA.

his father; the former possessed a large landed estate, mostly in Unst but also in Delting, whereas William's father John had bought land wherever he could, but principally in Yell, where his Annsbrae estate now comprised much of the north of the island.[6] William abandoned a fledgling career as advocate at law to come home and become a country gentleman; he had seen changing ways in the countryside transforming the Lowlands of Scotland, was now involved in managing his wife's Fife estate, and it seems that he was interested in fostering improvements in Shetland too. With his wife Eliza he settled at Gardie House, with a life's work before him and his notebooks filling up with comments on contemporary Shetland agriculture.

Whether William Mouat knew it or not, he was simply the latest in a line of observers with a professional interest in land management in Shetland. In 1769 William Balfour of Trenaby in Orkney had been appointed as factor by Sir Laurence Dundas, owner of the Lordship estates in Shetland, with instructions to investigate the state of his lands there and put them on a sound economic footing. Balfour's rental[7], drawn up in 1774 and completed in the early 1780s, is extensively annotated with a description of what he found in Shetland, having travelled from one end of the islands to the other, and investigated the status quo with the insight of a practical, intelligent Orcadian.

Balfour described the divisions of cultivated land in Shetland known as "touns" or towns. The ideal toun lay handy for the sea, with an adjacent scattald, which would provide peats for firing and grazing for livestock. Thus the toun of Brettabister in Nesting, although far from ideal in situation – "the arable, about 5 acres (but very indifferent soil), the pasture ground of small extent and far from good, the situation cold and windy" – was near the sea, "also [near to] the scattald and fine peats in it; and these conveniences contribute so much to the subsistence of the inhabitants, that this little spot, which could scarce make a possession for one family in Unst or Fetlar, has been for some time occupied by two, who contrive to live tolerable upon it." Unfortunately, such a favourable conjunction was far from being the norm. Thus Colvadeal and Meal in Unst, whose "mean and confined scattald" near the toun was "quite exhausted", could only supply "a wretched kind of firing instead of peats, of which they have none ..."

Touns were inhabited by one, or several, families and it is here that Balfour signals real trouble. It appears that as early as the 1770s, when smallpox was at last eradicated and the death rate began to fall[8] that population growth in Shetland, necessitating the subdivision of holdings, was beginning to undermine the sustainability of local communities, especially those on marginal land. Balfour's description of cause and effect, although written about Unst, applied, as he himself noted, to "most other parts of the country" (i.e. Shetland).

The wealth or poverty of the inhabitants consists chiefly, or arises from the produce of, their cattle and sheep. Wherever the inhabitants are numerous in proportion to the extent of common, a smaller proportion of these must fall to the share of each ... the splitting of possessions in the view of accommodating a greater number of fishermen, hath not produced the effect intended to any great degree, but hath produced others tending very much to increase the poverty of the inhabitants. Formerly a tenant who possessed 16 or 18 merks land, had besides 12 or 18 milk cows, 8 or 10 oxen worth 35/- to 50/- sterling each. They were necessary to plow his land, their dung contributed much to improve it, when old their skins furnished shoes, and the beef either meat to his family or money to pay his rent. In time of scarcity or famine which obliged him to contract debt, these with the sheep a more extensive common enabled him to keep, were a fund of credit, and by the product of his sheep and cattle he could discharge his debts in a short time, so that his misfortunes only stimulated his industry. His children too, seeing they had a reasonable expectation of succeeding to something upon his death, were encouraged to remain in his family, often to marry so as to have two, three or sometimes more families and of course as many fishermen in one house.

But when this farm came to be parcelled out into three or four possessions a fishermen who could buy perhaps the sixth share of an old boat and furnish perhaps a hired cow or two, with blankets to his bed and a pot to cook his victuals, had a competent stock to begin upon. He needed no oxen, for he and his wife could, with the assistance of a child or two, when grown up a little, delve their possession. If by unsuccessful fishing or bad crops, he contracted debt, it was nothing to him, for he had nothing to lose. If he was an able man, and could pull an oar, he knew the value sett upon him by the heritor to whom the whole profits of the fishing generally accrue, would induce him to supply his wants rather than want his fishing. And thus it became common for men who never had £100 Scots of stock to be 2 or £300, often more, in debt to their land lords, and to continue so all their lives.

The scattalds thus divided could keep but a few sheep for each possessor, and a few sheep are not worth the care and attention they require. The children probably starved in their infancy; as soon as they got over it would see that, their parents possessing nothing, they had

William Mouat

nothing to expect from them. Indigent for the present and hopeless for the future their situation could not be worse in any country, but there was a chance of bettering it abroad, and therefore they prudently hazarded that chance.

Splitting farms in this manner did at first indeed promote earlier marriages and these necessarily tended to increase population, but as the people were increased only to emigrate, the consequence is now considered by the most intelligent people of the country, simply as an exchange of a wealthy or substantial peasantry for perhaps a greater number of beggars. This is particularly the case in this island of Unst, and the neighbouring one of Fetlar, in neither of which there is now to be found one man of substance for 10 about 40 years ago. The people are perhaps more numerous, but the common stock of wealth is reduced at least two thirds, and there is not now in these islands, nor in all the country taken together, one yoke of oxen for six 50 years ago, and the sheep, though not in the same proportion perhaps, have also decreased in number amazingly, and must necessarily decrease, by the increased number of horses required to transport peats, for it will be obvious that two, three or four even of the smallest families, must consume a great deal more of peats, than would abundantly supply one of the largest. For which reason, if it were otherwise good management, to split and multiply possessions, it must be improper where firing is hard to be got, or by a long land carriage ... where that carriage must be performed by horses, otherwise of no use and totally unproductive.

Balfour noted how, on Littlaland, on the Finzie scattald in Fetlar:

...there is not much that is rich or good, yet it happens here as almost every where in Shetland, that the sole tenant of the town by superior industry lives better and pays his rent more punctually than those that possess so much better land in the towns of Finzie, Strand and Aith, where many tenants are crowded together and labour run rigg.[9] For it holds universally, the more extensive the town and the more farmers upon it, the poorer they are.

Circumstances could be much worse.

Framgord, in the division of the parish called Ashiness, contains 40 merk land ... the soil is good but the arable of very small extent, ... no scattald or peats, and the arable exposed to blasting (i.e. wind) exceedingly. These circumstances, with the number of towns crowded together in this corner, renders this the worst lands in the parish or perhaps in Shetland. The people, while they are young and vigorous, fish successfully, but run into debt nevertheless almost every year. By the time they are old they are only fit to be turned over by a tacksman

53

who is also proprietor of the lands, from his own to those of Sir Laurence Dundas, from which they pay no rent, let the houses, if he is admitted to have any, go to ruin and die beggars.

Balfour saw a remedy to some of these ills. In the parish of Tingwall the people of that country had formerly been obliged to go "20 or 30 miles from their home to ply the summer fishing". This was met with

> ... very great reluctance and consequently with as little success. After some experiments, it was deemed more expedient in consideration of a moderate advance in rent, the whole payable in money, to leave them entirely at liberty to fish or not as they pleased, and the effects are evident from the late improvements made on their lands, which may enable them some years hence to bear another rise of rent ...

He instanced a tenant at Kurkugairth (Tingwall), who, "since ... liberate from fishing, hath added 2 full acres of the worst pasture to his arable and made it tolerable land by carrying earth upon it".

There were, however, indications of trouble ahead. Burraland in Northmavine, a town of about 10 merks of land, provided livings to two families:

> ... arable ... about 7 acres, the soil well and inclining to moss. The meadow and pasture ground within dykes are, for the extent of land, pretty good, and there is a limestone quarry in them of some value to the tenants. The scattald is very extensive and all round the toun, for a mile or two, deep moss, so that except to good travellers it is only accessible in summer. Having access to the sea on both sides ... the tenants have almost every advantage from it that this country possesses. There are two good fishermen upon it, one possessed of a large stock of sheep, and two very good and large farmhouses put up almost entirely at their own expence." This situation appeared to be at risk. "Some late attempts have been to circumscribe them in the use of the scattald, with what justice is uncertain. But **they should be protected to the utmost extent of the right** (my emphasis) for here their sheep and their fishing materials make the bulk of their stock.

Balfour's concern was always that tenants should have the viability of their holdings protected; when tenants in Haglabister, with an alleged right of pasture on the east side of the voe towards Whiteness and Nesting, "say they have of late been disturbed", his view was again that "their right if they have any ought to be maintained".

Again and again Balfour saw the effects of overcrowding. At Gruton (Aithsting and Sandsting), the toun inhabitants were "a number of beggars crowded together and such can never derive any benefit from the scattald, because they can never possess any stock to use it". He distrusted tacksmen, who might impoverish the tenants to secure their own profit with no interest in the longer term.

In Tingwall where the new conditions of money rents and no services looked likely to bring prosperity "if the exactions or extortions of tacksmen do not check their industry" as Balfour pointed out:

> ... no good reason appears for exposing these tenants to any hardship of this kind, as the factor may with the utmost ease collect the rents of all the property rents upon the main island without the interposition of temporary extortioners ...

He argued the case for proper leases. At Stromfirth a dispute over the scattald

> ... ought to be enquired into, as the scattalds where they are extensive and commodious are the great support of the inhabitants, and now more valuable to Sir L Dundas' tenants in this quarter that they have tacks, which may render their possessions more permanent, for without a permanent possession the tenants can derive no benefit from the commons ...

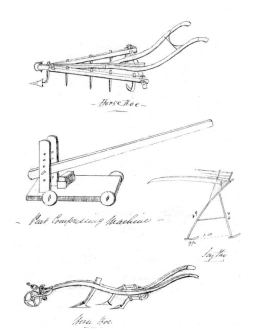

Sketches of innovative agricultural machinery of the time – two types of "horse hoe", a scythe, and a "peat compressing machine".

Balfour was in fact arguing for proper land management, with secure tenants enabled to benefit from their own efforts. Sheep farming, being "a work of much time and care", needed long leases to be successful, and he recognised that individuals needed security and time to build sustainable enterprises. The Scalloway islands, inhabited only because of the fishing, were on the edge of viability. Hence they should be let to "one man with a long lease, such as would stimulate industry to improve the fishing and perhaps the land". As for tacksmen, they too needed long leases to give them a vested interest in improving, otherwise "one who has only a lease for a few years hath only an interest but that of getting all he possibly can in the little time allowed for him". Balfour considered that landlords could act to eliminate extortion; improvement was then likely to follow, as it already had when fishing tenures were abolished.

As for tenants, their wellbeing was crucial. Southseater in Gulberwick he found "let to good tenants, free from all obligations except payment of a money rent; and all such tenants should be protected, especially at first, until experience hath showen whether this management is expedient, whether the rent is moderate, or otherwise".

At Housegord, an enviable holding with six acres "of the richest meadow ground in Shetland", the hay crop "in tolerable years" produced a surplus sufficient to pay a considerable part of the rent.

However he recorded instances where the land itself was so poor that living on it would always be problematic. At North Laxfirth, ground "long inhabited by beggars" had been freed by the landlord "from all burdens and prestations except a money rent", but whether the tenants would be able to pay it was questionable,"... so many bad crops and so close upon one another are against a fair experiment, but there is more against them from the small extent and mean quality of the lands ..."

At Trondray the tenants had at first reaped the benefits of their work.

> They have considerably more substance, cattle, sheep and fishing implements; they are better fed, better clothed and more comfortably lodged than they were ten years ago; and they seem to feel the change. Their industry now being for themselves and their families, they appear evidently animated to greater exertion ...

But this encouraging state of affairs was checked by crop failure in the 1780s, and the letting of the island to a tacksman "who will have his rent if the stock upon the land can pay him. Tho' by law no rent is due for these two crops, as they certainly (are) not equal to seed and labour. The cod fishing, one great resource, hath failed totally for two years." Balfour commented: "The consequences are obvious, if shocking to humanity."

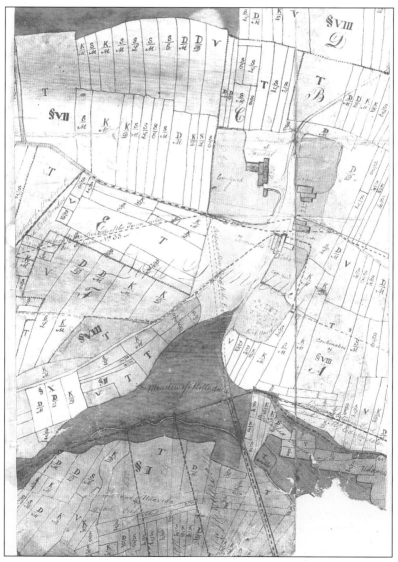

Part of a map showing the complex system of runrig cultivation in Norwick, Unst "as surveyed by T. Irvine, October and November 1822".

Balfour's assessment of Shetland emerges from the detailed picture he paints. He advocated responsible estate management, with long-term improvement kept in mind; he believed that the abolition of fishing tenures and other services, and the granting of leases, would free tenants to make the best of their holdings in their own interests, and consequently that of their landlord; and he pointed out the deleterious effects of asset-stripping. How far such innovations might have been attempted had they been widely canvassed in Shetland is hard to judge; dislike of innovation was by no means confined to one segment of island society, and passive resistance undermined the efforts of Hunter of Lunna to abolish his fishing tenures a few years later.

Balfour, however, had himself identified the other factors which were to thwart many well-intentioned efforts over the next century. The first was the pernicious effect of the growth of population, resulting in the sub-division of holdings; the second, even less amenable, the very marginal nature of much of Shetland's agricultural land. This was not Orkney, where better soils and the slightly warmer climate encouraged the development of agricultural skills and produced some of the best farmers in Britain.

Balfour, acquainted with the sour peaty soils of Yell and the rocky braes of Eshaness, also knew what had happened even in areas where better land had not of itself been enough to avoid disaster. An ever-growing population lacking skills in animal or crop husbandry and attempting to work poor land was a recipe for struggle at best and famine at worst. Balfour's belief in viable agricultural units begged the question of the surplus population, a quandary which was to bedevil the following century.

Balfour was succeeded as factor to Lord Dundas by John Bruce of Sumburgh, and Bruce in his turn by Thomas Bolt of Cruister in Bressay. In the early 1790s Bolt was instructed once again to review the Lordship rental and report to his employer. Thomas Bolt was an old friend of the Mouats, of course; whether or not he discussed contemporary problems with them is not certain, though it seems extremely probable. At all events, a copy of the Lordship rental and Bolt's notes thereon was discovered in a ledger belonging to John Mouat (it has a neat little leather nameplate on the front). Twenty years after Balfour, Bolt's remarks, although less voluminous, corroborate his predecessor's view of

Shetland agriculture and attest to a dismal failure to act in the face of gathering difficulty

Bolt's careful inventory of lands from Unst to Dunrossness together with the taxes due on them, shows how little had changed since Balfour's day. Rents payable in a combination of oil, butter and (Scots) money produced endless, often acrimonious, disputes; Bolt himself, having been seen off by the Unst heritors – only James Spence, the owner of Uyea, paid an exclusively money rent – gratefully recorded how the Fetlar heritors "pay the Minister a settled annual sum for these (corn) teinds, and that without the least dispute or cavil about the money". He also noted the power of custom in profoundly conservative communities: Mr Bruce of Urie in Fetlar paid "what he and his predecessors have for more than a century paid," which was, as Bolt estimated, about half what he actually owed. Bolt discovered other errors in the Fetlar rental: "... scatt, wattle, ox and sheep money inserted in Mr Balfour's Rentall above what ever had been paid in the memory of man and which he never could get payment of, and did discompt to the people at acompting with them, but did not correct his rental".

The modern farm steading at Keldabister, Bressay, built by William Mouat at the site of the old toun. The buildings and layout are unchanged from 1820, except for the large building to the right, a new silo. The photograph, taken in 1970, shows oats in the stackyard for the last time. Henceforth winter feed was provided by silage, a twentieth century agricultural improvement.

But in spite of Bolt's own observations the Shetland mindset remained wedded to the past:

> Lerwick 5 June 1795. All the lands ... [in Whiteness and Weisdale] mentioned are sett in tack to the Tenants at the above rent from crop 1795 payable 1796, exclusive of the scatt which they are to pay conform to the scatt rental. All the tenants except Mr Ross and the tenants in Tubie and Nisbister have tacks for 5 years & are not obliged to go to the fishing, or any other services; nor are they to be removed while they pay their rents in Butter and money as above stated, or the current country price for the butter, in case of not paying in kind. That part of the kelp shores formerly sett of[f] to the tenants for manure is reserved to them. When the tacks held by Magnus Erasmeson & John Ross expire, the factor for the time should charge the antient Butter rent upon the lands deducting the same from the present money rental 6/- Sterling per Lispond.
>
> Stroholm (72 merks) ... .there never has been more than 69 merks land found under this Room. The butter and oil payments have ever been disputed and never paid but for the 69 merks land they pay 10/- Scots per merk.
>
> ... the keeping up of the Butter and Oil demands on all these lands [is] tending only to create disputes betwixt the tacksmen and the tenants and betwixt the factor and the tacksman. To avoid all cause of difference and dispute, the factor thinks it more for the interest of all to restrict the rental to the money payments above stated which it is contended has been the immemorial use and wont of payment.

In Aithsting and Sandsting:

> Mr William Balfour altered all the payments of the landmails of the above property lands, and abolished all Butter payments and sett the lands for a neat money rent, the scatt, wattle, ox and sheep money included, and also abolished any obligation on the tenants for Fishing, and every servitude, and on these terms the present tenants hold the lands ...
>
> Lerwick 21 March 1801. Thereafter the factor found that it was more for the interest of Lord Dundas as well as better for the tenants also to revive the antient Butter Rent and he deducted them at the conversions stated at being £3-6/- Scots per Lispond of Butter and 12/- per can of oil from the money rent as fixed by Mr Balfour...

Other rentals reinforce the picture of a complex, chaotic and disputatious state of affairs. The parish rental of Bressay, Burra and

Quarff (July 1800) differed internally – Bressay paid corn teind in butter and oil and land rents to the heritors in Scots money; in Burra all payments were in Scots money; and in Quarff corn teinds were in Scots money, and landrents to the heritors were partly in butter and partly in Scots money. The 1786 Delting rents were paid in butter and Scots money, as was Unst in 1790 and North Yell in 1807. A Bressay rental of 1804 describes how corn teind, "payable by the possessors of the lands where laboured only" was due in butter and oil; scat and wattle in Scots money; but the rental itself was computed in Sterling. Within the small island of Bressay itself the townships of Aith and Gunelsta paid corn teind at a different rate to the rest of the island, and only in butter (1811).

When Samuel Hibbert wrote his book about Shetland about 30 years after Bolt wrote his notes – it was published in 1822 – he described Shetland agriculture as "debased"[10], giving many depressing examples, and his description of the effects of fishing tenures, to wit, a state of dependency "too often the forerunner of an inactive and unadventurous state of poverty," is a terrible warning to any small community where dependency, by whatever agency, is fostered. Its effects in Shetland were obvious. During the long wars with France the Shetland economy had benefited from the wartime market for salt and dried fish at good prices, and from the remittances paid to the wives of the men serving in the Royal Navy. When peace finally came after Napoleon's defeat at Waterloo in 1815, boom was succeeded by post-war slump. The labour market was flooded with returning ex-servicemen. In Shetland their fishing skills at least meant they could earn a living; but Shetland still relied on subsistence agriculture, like the fishing dangerously susceptible to bad years, and now confronted by, and palpably unequal to, the task of feeding a steadily increasing population. In 1812 William Mouat estimated that about one quarter of the populace were children under eight years of age.

Mouat's detailed analysis of contemporary Shetland agriculture show it to have been primitive, inflexible, out-of-date and, psychologically carrying the burden of Hibbert's "unadventurous dependency", generally afraid of new ideas. "The climate [is] too much urged as an objection to [agricultural] improvement" he noted.[11]

Land was often worked runrig, a system described by Balfour as long ago as 1774 – the rigs "in so many spots, and so much intersected with grass, that their extent cannot be known except by an actual survey".[12]

But as William Mouat noted:

> ... the tenants have a strong prejudice in its favour. Its advantages are – the common interest in the crop, necessary in a state of imperfect inclosure. The equal division of the different qualities of land to tenants who have no notion or wish for improvement. These advantages are real.

Set against this his notes reveal the practices which runrig was powerless to alleviate: the tyranny of "doing or leaving undone simply because it has been so done or left undone before";[13] no enclosure so that arable land lay vulnerable to stock throughout the winter, no winter herding, no souming[14] "except what necessity dictates" (a recipe for gross overgrazing), little understanding of natural manures (where they were used, like seaweed, often "two thirds of the good of them lost"), crops generally sown too late ("early harvest is the desirable object") and, worse than anything else and "productive of much calamity", the lack of winter and spring feed for livestock.

Mouat did not approve of the subdivision of holdings but outsets were acceptable, significantly, "because they afford additional means of subsistence". The archaic systems for rents paid in kind or in days' works he thought should be abolished, pointing out local differences in practice. (Bressay "casualties" were three days works, "generally defined and known, very seldom produce ... almost always in labour of some kind. In some places however arbitrary services are exacted. Quendal makes tenants thrash the crop and teind corn.")

New ideas involved enclosure to protect crops, better animal husbandry, and the use of turnips for winter feed. All of these were encouraged by the Shetland Society, formed in 1815 by a group of landowners wishing to encourage agricultural improvement in the islands. William Mouat, secretary, was responsible for the Society's annual reports, which, from 1815 onwards, chronicle the Society's work. There was much to do. The Society found poor management of the infield, no crop rotation, and crops overgrown with weeds – to have bere oats "free from weeds is not yet known". Trials of sown grasses were attempted in Tingwall but were useless without enclosure since "all the stock in the neighbourhood have free access to it during winter". The Shetland breed of sheep, regarded probably as the only breed suitable for its tough environment, had suffered so much that "partly from inherent defects, and perhaps principally from neglect and mismanagement, [it] has become so unproductive that there is hardly any change, which, for a time at least, will not be an improvement".

FERRYMAN'S COTTAGE, BRESSAY.

This 1869 drawing by J. T. Reid shows Northerhouse at Noss Sound, Bressay.

There was a response to the initiative: Society membership rose from sixteen founder members to forty-eight; entry to its annual competitions, run exclusively for "common udallers and tenants", from three in the first year to thirty the next. Plainly there were, within contemporary Shetland, those for whom living on the edge encouraged resoucefulness and the ability to turn a hand to anything. In October 1816 Thomas Jamieson, tenant in Aithsness, Sand, received £3-10/- as cash prize for a crop of ½ acre of turnips, with the comment "a stranger to the system of improved husbandry but is anxious for information; he is very active, has greatly extended his arable ground, built fences at great expense and personal labour, and done much more than could have been expected, considering he has no lease". James Mitchell, on an outset near Aith, was commended for harvesting "as fine oats as they had seen, ground under crop for the first year, well laid out and produce excellent". Mitchell had built a house and enclosed ground with no assistance from the proprietor. He held it rent free for the first ten years and thereafter only a small rent was to be charged; the Society gave him a cash donation.

Prizes were offered to encourage the production of turnips, valuable as winter feed, and "artificial grasses" (ryegrass and clover) for improved pasturage; for the breaking out of "waste ground"; and for improved breeding stock – bulls, stallions and rams. In addition the society issued pamphlets about new techniques, and from their own resources engaged a cartwright and blacksmith to come to Shetland to supply agricultural implements. These men were given free houses and workshops for three years while they established their trade.

The men who ran the Shetland Society were private individuals; they invested their own money to fund its operations; they saw how the "want of capital among the tenantry must retard improvements," and some perhaps glimpsed Balfour's thesis that a prosperous tenantry benefited the entire community. But the Society did not last, perhaps under the burden of the sustained effort required, perhaps also because there was no democracy to give it credibility. There was no local organisation with the status to bring about change, which, however beneficial, is likely always to be resisted. Local government in Scotland was then still entirely unreformed, and as no Shetlander had a vote in Parliamentary elections, the ability of the islands to help themselves was curtailed.[15]

Change was to come piecemeal. Arthur Gifford of Busta had advocated the granting of leases, to give stability and encourage forward planning. Thomas Mouat had been doing so selectively since the turn of the century, for time scales up to nineteen years; normally the areas involved were larger than the 6 ½ merks land in Unst "be south the voe," liferented in 1805 to L. Bartholmson.

The status of the small farms, not yet called crofts, was more problematic. These were theoretically let annually, so giving no incentive to improve, but were often held for long periods, thus neatly achieving the worst of all possible arrangements, and they usually had no lease at all.

Nonetheless there is evidence that the tenants themselves were well aware of the benefits of enclosure. William Mouat's accounts detail extensive dyke-building in both Unst and Bressay, where the men of Ham and Kirkabister built 354 fathom of new dykes and repaired existing ones in the winter of 1822-23, for which they were paid at the rate of 10d per fathom (interestingly wages in Unst were much lower: Magnus Winwick building the dyke at Gue in Balliasta, was paid 4 ½ d per fathom). Mouat regularly paid extra to valued workers, with more than a hint that the cup that cheers was as appreciated then as it is now. Matthew Nelson and William Morrison each received 20/- at New Year 1820, and the Manson family, who had supplied lime, were paid 4/- "for a dram." In March that year Laurence Anderson was paid for "building, quarrying and carting" stone for the new dyke at the Veing, high above the sea cliffs in the south of Bressay; a week previously William Mouat had walked out to see the works completed, and dispensed "handsels" there to the men.

As well as dykes there was money spent on roads – to the Voehead in Bressay in February 1822 – on repairs to tenants' houses and byres, on outsets, and on new buildings, like the mill at Snarravoe in south Unst in 1820. As William Mouat took over from his elders – his uncle Thomas died in 1819 and his father John in 1824 – the estate accounts reveal a multi-faceted business including whale oil, cooperage, whales, boats. The 1841 Statistical Account describes how Mouat had built at Uyeasound in Unst "a lodge for his accommodation, when he visits that part of his property which lies in Unst: and a range of neat houses along the shore of the harbour, for dwellinghouses; a shop for merchandise; warehouses; and workshops for a blacksmith, boat-carpenters, and a cooper".

Lerwick as seen from Annsbrae in 1806, copied from the original drawing by M. A. Cameron in 1885. Annsbrae faces north, looking towards Unst, the birth island of its owner, John Mouat.

This busy effort was founded on the strong contemporary belief, certainly shared by William Mouat, that economic prosperity depended upon a large population; and the corollary, also acknowledged by him, that agricultural improvement, carrying as it did the necessity of abolishing runrig and consolidating holdings, implied a proportion of people for whom subsistence farming would no longer be possible.

In his 1815 notes he wrote:

> [There are] no large farms, at least in rent, in extent some of them perhaps might be advantageously diminished, that is to say in extent of hill pasture. Large farms would probably diminish the population in the first instance though as surely as they increase productiveness they would in the end increase it or at least increase the comforts of the same number and diminish the number of the poor ...

If people were displaced, then alternative employment had to be found, and this difficult necessity seems to have driven Mouat's expensive programme of economic infrastructure. There was some development – chromate in Unst from 1820s and the stone quarries in Bressay, where men learnt the skills which gave them a name for mason work and the ability to earn a living building Lerwick.

William Mouat ran his business from Gardie House. He established a home farm at Keldabister, replacing the old toun with a modern farm steading and importing a grieve from Fife to run it. The newly enclosed parks, symmetrically laid out with neat stone dykes, form part of the designed landscape which centres on Gardie House, and marry beauty with utility. The thorn hedge, planted like thousands of others in farm roads up and down Scotland, was carefully tended, its maintenance part of the farm lease from 1842 onwards. But the farm was not a rich man's toy; the high costs of its establishment had to be recouped, and, competently run by a succession of able grieves[16], its oats and bere crops were regularly sent to Gorgie Mills by Edinburgh and returned as meal, the surplus of which was a cash crop. The farm gave employment to local men and also those who came north for work – in November 1828 James Nisbet had his passage paid to Shetland (it cost £1-10/-). His wages were £30 per year in cash, plus 6 ½ bolls oatmeal, one pint of milk per day, and free house and fire, no doubt in the bothy which adjoins the grieve's cottage.

Keldabister farm, in hand and on good land, was a viable enterprise, but without careful consideration the establishment of farms meant a debit account in money as well as human terms. In 1834 Mouat had turned the touns of Lumbister and Vollaster in North Yell into a grazing and sheep farm run for him by John Forsyth, a shepherd from south. The property was too small, however, to return a profit as well as two men's wages, and the land lay unoccupied until 1852.[17] The failure of the Vollaster farm coincided with the bad weather and hardship of the late 1830s; lessons might have been drawn from this experience by all concerned.

NOTES:

1   Fouthie – prosperous, having abundance, from Scots fouth, abundance, plenty.
2   Hjaltland Miscellany Vol 1.
3   William Mouat, notebooks, Gardie House Archive.
4   Tacksman – a chief tenant, who leased land directly from the landowner and had the right to collect its revenue.
5   *Shetland Merchant's Daybook*, 1762.
6   GHA 1852/21.
7   SA ref D 311/22.
8   William P. L. Thomson, *Population and Depopulation in Shetland and the Outside World 1469-1969*, ed Donald Withrington, Aberdeen University Study Series no 157.
9   run rigg – a system of joint landholding, whereby each tenant had rigs (strips) of land allocated by lot each year, giving each in turn a share of the better land.
10   Samuel Hibbert, *A Description of the Shetland Islands*, 1822.
11   The identical excuse was more than once advanced to the present writer regarding gardening in Shetland in the 1960s.
12   Lands in Westsandwick, Yell, and Brough, North Delting.
13   Shetland Society Annual report, 1820.
14   souming – the fixed number of animals which may be supported on a given area of ground.
15   No Shetlander had a right to vote in Parliamentary elections before the franchise was enlarged in the Reform Act of 1832, a situation keenly resented. Robert Hunter of Lunna (1778-1833) was prominent amongst those in Shetland who saw the need for reform. He was one of those who spent months in London before and during the passage of the bill, persuading, explaining and lobbying for reform. The 1832 Reform Act enfranchised every proprietor with a rental of over £10; in the north isles the electorate jumped to 275 in Orkney and Shetland instead of under 30, all in Orkney.
16   Grieve – foreman or manager.
17   *Lonely, lovely Lumbister* – Robert L. Johnson, Shetland Life, January 1987.

CHAPTER FOUR

YOUNG WILLIAM

We are truly sorry to hear the severe gale of Wednesday the 11th has done so much mischief in Zetland – and the more so that the sufferers are not likely to receive such liberal aid from England etc as they have done during this summer.
Captain William Cameron, Edinburgh, to W.M.C. Mouat, Shetland, 25 October 1837.

When William Mouat returned to Shetland with his wife Eliza Cunningham in 1812 it was with the intention of living in Gardie House. "I am resolved," he wrote, "to give the house a thorough repair to fit it for my own residence." In the face of his uncle Thomas Mouat's tartly expressed belief that the house was too grand for "merely a tacksman of Bressay,"[1] William displayed, not for the first or the last time in his career, a total imperviousness to anything except getting his own way. Gardie House, unlived in since the death of James Henderson in 1797, was certainly in need of repair and renovation – as late as 1818 the house insurance account mentions that it was still "roofed partly with slates and partly with paper".

William Mouat, however, had much greater ambitions. Scion of a family almost unique in Shetland in their interest in matters architectural[2], he was in addition now familiar with the beauty of Edinburgh's New Town, where he and Eliza had begun their married life. Eliza herself brought her own style to Shetland; raised in conditions of comfort and elegance, and marrying a like-minded husband, ("it will

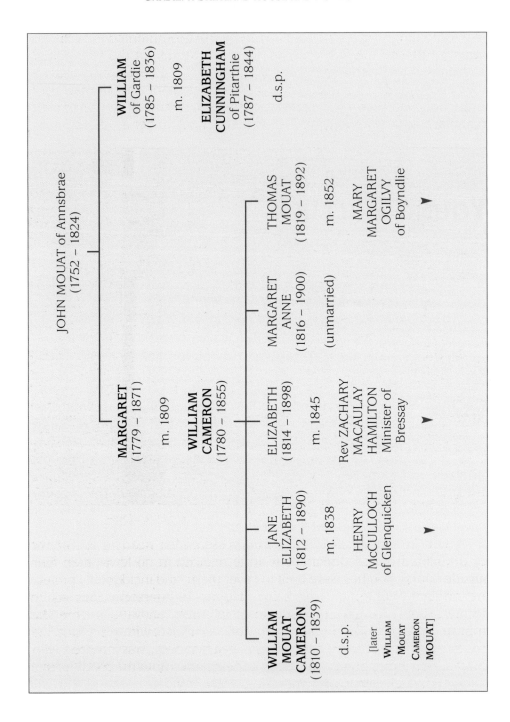

take something to keep them", her mother had commented to William's father John), she was not likely to accept anything but the best. Eliza's contribution to the rescue of Gardie House over the next twenty years is nowhere recorded (the fate of the female half of the human race throughout most written history), but the programme of improvements in and around the house probably owed as much to her as to him.

The front porch at Gardie House, added c. 1812 by William and Eliza Mouat.

There were practicalities to be addressed: after nearly a century of icy draughts from all directions (Gardie rejoiced in no fewer than four outside doors), porches were built to cover them, and incidentally protect the original moulding carved by Magnus Henderson's masons to decorate his principal entrance. Internally the renovations bore the imprint of Classical Edinburgh; a new main staircase, with graceful stone treads rising round three sides of the staircase well, was finished with delicate but strong iron balusters, and the doorway into the hall lit with a beautiful fanlight whose derivation is obvious.

rom Edinburgh too came the furniture to fill the empty rooms, and the china, glass, and other household articles that a wealthy young couple needed for daily use. The Henderson writing room became a library with built-in shelves (behind which the original green paint peeps to this day), to house William Mouat's growing collection of books and, on the diningroom walls, family portraits were hung, not only as a statement of prestige, but more subtly, to reinforce the Enlightenment agenda of the rational man: serious, purposeful and authoritative, undoubtedly a persona dear to William Mouat's heart and one that in some respects truly described him.

The drawingroom at Gardie House photographed in the 1990s.

Servants looked after the house. They carried the fuel that warmed the rooms and the water for washing and cleaning. Good servants were ardently sought, hard to find, harder still to keep. A male "house servant" supervised domestic operations, a job which necessarily implied a degree of trust and was, therefore, very well paid. Robert Milne, who came into service in November 1826, was paid £45 yearly, far more than the working grieve at Keldabister farm, John Bell, whose wages that same year were £22 (though they rose to £30 in 1831), or the gardener John

Robertson, paid £25 and 6 bolls of meal. However, Milne left less than a year later, to the Mouats' regret – "a good servant," noted William Mouat, "but nervous and fancied he did not agree with Shetland". It proved difficult to find the right person for the post. In May 1829 Laurence Stout was engaged, but he did not last either, though in this case it seems that he failed to perform. He was discharged less than a year later as "old and failed, and conceited".

The backbone of the domestic labour force consisted of local girls, who worked for their keep and cash wages paid quarterly. Amounts varied, but were not high – the totals were all below £10 per annum. It was usual, however, to give them small amounts extra, and if the lass was leaving to get married, and had given satisfaction, then the bonus reflected this. Betty Morrison, "a very good servant", received the equivalent of half a year's wages (15/-) when she left to marry William Smith of Aith. Some girls working at Gardie, a focal point of activity with visitors of many sorts from social to practical, met their future husbands there. Jenny Hunter "went away with credit" when she married the wheelwright Robert Davidson, and Martha Gillie[3], who had come to work at Gardie House in the early 1830s, later married the gardener William Edgar. (Edgar was the son of John Edgar, the Berwickshire farmer who had been brought to Shetland by William Mouat to run the farm of Setter on the east side of Bressay. William had started work as a garden apprentice (at a wage of 4/6 per week) in 1833, so he and Martha had known each other for some time. When he began work, aged 13, he was living at home, and walked across Bressay twice every day to and from work.[4] But it was a chance to learn a skill, and Edgar took his chance. By 1841 he had become gardener in his turn and had the little cottage beside the North Garden at Gardie; he and Martha married in 1844, and, part of a quiet exodus to the opportunities of the town, left Bressay for Lerwick, where Edgar became a merchant and a Wesleyan Methodist preacher.[5])

At Gardie House good behaviour was expected. The Mouats did not tolerate sexual misconduct among the servants: if discovered, it resulted in immediate dismissal, whether or not the girl was pregnant. Both James Smith, house servant in 1827-28, and Agatha Henderson had to leave when their liaison came to light, Smith "turned off without a character or warning". Agatha went south, to be followed later by her sister Jean, whose bonus was more generous than Agatha's, reflecting the Mouats' opinions of both girls. But Jeany Henderson, the dairymaid, disappears from the records, "sent away with child to J Laurenson".

Such firmness probably reassured the more responsible mothers in the community, who would not wish their daughters to go into service where standards were lax or they might be preyed upon by a male employer (a circumstance not entirely unknown in Shetland)[6]. It seems likely that Eliza Mouat insisted upon the standards that her own family – her mother was a Gordon – expected of their servants.

Outside the house other workers are recorded – the dairymaid Kitty Manson, who replaced the erring Jeany Henderson; Marion Cowwife, who earned 8/-, later 9/- a quarter; and a succession of gardeners, whose wages, like the farm grieve's, were regularly raised (always an indication of valued skilled workers). Daniel Brims' wages rose from £26 to £30 during his 5 years at Gardie (he left in 1831). His successor, George James, was paid £26 but with several in kind additions – free house and firing, 6 bolls meal, 1 pint of milk per day, 30 bushel potatoes, and his passage paid to Shetland; he remained in post at least till 1834.

There was plenty for gardeners to do. Around the house walled gardens were established and the remains of most of the old houses swept away (though one booth survived as a storage shed, and the frontage of Anne Gray's little house is still to be seen, incorporated into the garden wall). The original Henderson garden to the north-east of Gardie was transformed, sheltered behind its new high wall, a prime situation for growing produce for the house with a lean-to hothouse for fruit and flowers. Vents through the wall admitted heat from the boilerhouse on the north side. The stone flags for the hothouse were supplied from Aith by Gilbert Laurenson, whose tenancy of the quarries there added supplemented his income from his farm at Uphouse, high on the hillside looking down over Bressay Sound.

Other features included walks and terraces, flights of dressed stone steps, a sunken lawn, an arched gateway and a beautifully constructed stone-lined water channel. A cottage was built for the gardener and, in keeping with the improving agenda, many trees were planted. All this created a green oasis, a favourite place for contemporaries to visit. Charlton, writing in 1834, described the gardens, bright with tulips in spring, a place of peace and seclusion. "During the summer months, when the harbour is crowded with foreign vessels, the Dutch sailors

An example of the beautiful stonework created in the grounds of Gardie House by William Mouat's skilled stonemasons.

frequently come to walk in this garden ... nothing is ever injured here by these quiet inoffensive foreigners ..." [7]

Plants are transitory; infrastructure remains. The improvements carried out by William and Eliza Mouat during their tenure can be seen today. Gardie House was fortunate indeed that their taste was equal to the challenge. The old Henderson mansion was transformed into the graceful building set in designed grounds that can be seen today, a setting for William and Eliza Mouat to live the life that suited them. Their entertaining set the social tone. Every notable visitor to Shetland anticipated the invitation to dine at Gardie, to admire the house and gardens, to taste the grapes and peaches from the hothouse. Sir Walter Scott, an old friend of John Mouat, visited in 1814. Captain Ross, commissioned by the Admiralty to find the elusive north-west passage, called in on his way north in 1818 to be entertained and sent on his way with a bullock for fresh beef. The expedition was unsuccessful, but survived to return safely, and Captain Ross presented William Mouat with a narwhal's horn some 7ft long, which is still in the house.

Only one imperfection marred the lengthening years – no babies arrived. They would have been no doubt welcome enough, but their absence does not seem to have caused profound grief. William and Eliza had a facile fondness for the enlarging family of William's half-sister Margaret, and as those children grew up, they came on visits and brought their own youthful vitality to brighten the lives of their aunt and uncle.

Such a visit came in the autumn of 1823, when the Mouats' nephew, William Mouat Cameron, then aged 11, visited them for an extended stay. Young William was the eldest child of Margaret Mouat and her husband, Captain William Cameron, whose Army career had ended with the outbreak of peace in 1815. The Camerons had come home to Shetland and now lived at Belmont in Unst, Margaret's childhood home, and it was there that the five children grew up.

Captain and Mrs Cameron, living on an Army pension, were grateful for the financial assistance of the childless Mouats with the education of their elder son, although as so often with William Mouat, the reality did not quite square with the expectation and the Camerons found themselves still liable for £200. Mrs Cameron had never been close to her half-brother. The relationship was not an easy one; still, for the sake of the children, harmony was maintained. It was not unreasonable to assume, and hope was strengthened by comment made, that young William, well brought up, mature for his years, the apple of his mother's eye, evidently had a future in his uncle's empire.

The journal that William kept during his stay at Gardie and sent home regularly certainly contains frequent references to the kind treatment afforded him by his uncle and aunt. Perhaps this was to reassure his parents, for William all his life was sensitive to the feelings of others, whether openly expressed or not. He learned to cope with homesickness, perhaps betrayed by his frequent references to his baby brother "Tin Tom", for whom he spent time on the lathe making a wooden top; and he worried about his mother's health – "I hope Mammie's headacks [sic] are better". He recorded how, as the mornings grew darker and colder, he was given a candle to light his way, and porridge for breakfast "as the bread and milk kept me cold." A good breakfast would certainly have been helpful in coping with the curriculum which his uncle set him so that his education was not neglected: daily lessons began at 8 o'clock with Euclid (i.e. geometry), followed by "10 Latin, 11 ancient history, 2 French... 7 Arithmetic and my Journal". Later geography and chemistry were added to the curriculum. "I should very much like to understand Chemistry", he commented; and Dr Spence, who William had met in Lerwick, entered into the spirit of things (perhaps young William, like his father, had a likeable personality) and suggested to the boy's grandfather that the peat house at Annsbrae should be fitted up as a laboratory.

Life at Gardie House could not but seem very different from the cheerful hubbub of family life at Belmont, but his aunt and uncle enjoyed the novelty of his visit and in their own way made him welcome. His aunt outfitted him with new clothes and his uncle had a swing hung in the barn. With them he attended church, where Mr Barclay preached "with a great deal of action" and afterwards "went to the manse where we dined and drank tea. The boat was to have come for us but did not, and we walked home." He was taken to Lerwick where at Annsbrae he visited his grandfather John Mouat, now an old man, sick and failing and, alas, past fitting out laboratories for likely lads; William, however, was also interested in the shipping in the harbour.

> Yesterday I was on board [the *Norna*] but I think the *Fidelity* is better fitted than she ... her sailing seems to have been improved by her schoonership as a passage of 40 hours [from Leith] is very short. Mr Hay has some of the vessels which used to be in Grandfather's dock[8]. The London cod smack after having waited a day or two for an entrance, went to Mr Hay's[9] where there was rather deeper water.

But what young William enjoyed most, and took every opportunity to do, was to go up to the farm (he was used to doing this at home) and meet the men who worked there. He tagged along with them, helped when he could, listened to their talk and asked endless questions. He said goodbye to the farm servant Mathew Neilson, who after years of service "went for a sailor" with the Archangel brig; he learnt the details of his uncle's seven new cows – they cost £8-16 – and the trouble there was in swimming the two oxen he sold across the water to Lerwick. He heard how "the discovery ships the first day they were in got 40lb of onions for their broth pot and they used them at one boiling". He quizzed the farm grieve John Law about crop succession and ways of improving land, techniques now being put into practice at Keldabister. He watched Law

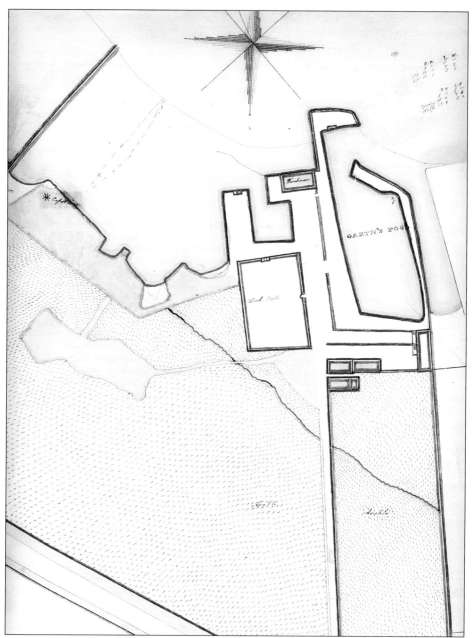

A map, drawn by Andrew D. Mathewson in 1832, of Garthspool, the dock in Lerwick built by John Mouat of Annsbrae.

making baskets and decided to learn "so that if ever I am cast on the desert isle (he had been reading Robinson Crusoe), I may be the basket maker rather than the useless gentleman."

There were Halloween festivities at Gardie House when William and the servants enjoyed the novelty of a magic lantern show:

> ... none of the servants here had seen it, they were highly delighted. Robert was sent to tell them to come and what he roared out was 'let anyone that wants to see the devil on Halloween come here' at which you may be sure they were in the greatest amazement, dropping eggs, burning nuts (although some of them when they had got their nuts ate them), dipping in the milk and water etc and they concluded by a hearty supper of bread, cheese, apples and porter.

The following weekend brought the celebration of Harvest Home. He wrote to his parents:

> The barn at Keldabister was cleared out early in the day and seats were made around the barn and about 6 o'clock the company began to arrive and they then began reels. Andrew Bruce came here last night and as he came just in time Aunty sent him up, though not exactly in ball costume, and he was among the bravest of them. Old Sanders Bolt, if you recollect him, was there and he too was dancing. About 11 o'clock supper came in which consisted of roast and boiled beef, roast and boiled fowls, and rice pudding in abundance with ale, beer and toddy etc. I left them about 12 o'clock but they kept it up till near 3 o'clock.

Nearly ten years later William Mouat Cameron kept another journal. By this time he was in his early twenties and, fresh from university education in Edinburgh, was in Shetland universally regarded as his uncle's heir, a situation which his aunt and uncle did nothing to discourage. But by now William Mouat's finances were beginning to cause him anxiety. Years of spending on both house and estate, coupled with a lavish lifestyle, were draining the pot of gold left him by his uncle Thomas, and as he himself well knew, the financial returns from the lands that he owned were small, and not getting any bigger, as the impulse to agricultural improvement failed to spread. His correspondence with his Edinburgh agent began to harp on the necessity of fundraising. William Mouat does not appear ever to have considered retrenchment. On the contrary, the public front was carefully

Gardie House as it would have looked at the time of William Mouat and his nephew, from a watercolour painted by Miss Rose Gamble in 1901.

maintained, the foreign holidays and the confident persona serving to maintain the impression of boundless resources.

It is unknown, and unknowable, how much William Mouat confided in his wife – possibly Eliza, sunny and charming as long as everything was fine, proved less reliable in the face of problems which could not indefinitely be sidetracked. He certainly did not make any suggestion of trouble looming to his young nephew, but used him as a general factotum in estate work; in particular they had set up a "copartnery" to run the fish business. It was a somewhat one-sided agreement – young William did all the work for rather little reward. However, in the winter of 1832, with financial anxieties beginning to weigh ever more upon William Mouat, he despatched young William to Ireland to look for new markets.

For a young man such a trip promised to satisfy a natural interest in new places and people, though it began in familiar enough territory.

Staying in Edinburgh at the beginning of the trip – 2nd January 1832 – William found that cholera was "on the increase at Haddington, soon expected at Edinburgh, not much dread apparently felt of it ..." and it certainly did not impair his enjoyment of a musical evening: "beautiful music seemed...to the enjoyment of an almost new sense. If ever I marry must have a musical woman. Great fool James Kinnear marrying just of age – marriages are said to be made in heaven but his in Orkney."

He travelled to Glasgow to embark for Belfast, finding himself in company with a large party of the 47th Regiment, whose officers entertained him with stories of campaigning in Burma; but he noticed "the shifts the poor soldiers' wives were put to, many with infants. No soldier should marry, nor anyone else till he can do as he chuses [sic] ..."

Arrival at Belfast saw the vessel:

> ... surrounded with boats and boarded with all sorts of people offering their services, [it] put me in mind of Brassa – *"A porter with a ticket please your honour"*, *"would your honour be so good as prefer the Commercial Hotel - best hotel in town your honour"*. Can't say much of the respectability of the first Irishes I have seen – if he had a hat he wanted one of his shoes, or if he had both arms to his coat the chances were he wanted one or both tails to it. One and all seemed to have a devil me care sort of face and many of them a most humorous and ready to laugh sort of expression to boot. The soldier on guard preventing a woman selling oranges coming on board, with a most inimitable expression she said *"and its prevent a poor woman selling oranges you would may you go to the devil and it's do it you will."* Wished very much for a companion to speak to – nowhere so solitary as unknowing and unknown in a crowd ... wished for Copland or my Aunt.

Later, travelling down to Dublin he saw the countryside "in good cultivation. Less so as we came further south. Lots of pigs upon the roads. Much fear as we came south of the White Boys; met with some Tipperary men, one a proprietor in the county, talking so coolly of the burning and plundering of the Tipperary people...never met such bloodthirstiness, the Orange against the Catholics." In Dublin he had a chance to meet and talk to Catholics – "how absurd the ideas some people have of RC's – very like other people ... don't even think less of them for being of a different religion" – but was less impressed by their religious services.

> ... how far far superior is the English service to the Catholic, no mummery, no part acted by the priests in which the people cannot partake. Much as I admire the music and some parts of the service of the Catholic chapel, it cannot for a moment be put in competition with the sensible and feeling service of the English church ...

On the road heading to the west he was interested to see:

> ... an iligant [sic] lady stop at a man building a wall on the roadside and ask if he had any commands for Dublin ... Was told that it was quite the practice for ladies particularly going to Dublin from the country to do any little commissions that the poor people they knew wished done and bring them from town with them ...

Again he observed the hatred between the Orangemen and the Catholics, and the universal belief among the Catholic population that repeal of the union with Great Britain would usher in utopia.

> ... the more I see of the Catholics, and it is altogether among them that I have been, I am aware how strong is the desire for a repeal of the Union.[10] Like most theorists they nourish like a favourite child their darling idea, and did it take place tomorrow I am pretty sure much disappointment would ensue ...

He described the verdant countryside near Limerick:

> ... where the very hedgerows were lines of trees, and the brambles made shoots of extraordinary length. But with all the advantage of climate and soil the management was very poor indeed – saw many true Irish cottages with a little potato ground of perhaps quarter of an acre in which generally a pig or two was very busy. The lang bed system seems to be very universal – beds not wider than 4 or 5 feet on which the potatoes are thrown broadcast. The cottages about twenty feet by ten or so, built of clay wrought with straw of rushes tapering considerably to the wall top and thatched with straw or rushes – when white washed and neatly kept they present a very neat appearance but this is not often the case ...

The countryside, in spite of natural fertility, he found "badly drained and ill cultivated" and the moorland "worse than the worst of Yell".

The high point of the trip was the lakes of Killearney: "a view, but such a glorious view, oh ye powers of brightness, such a view as neither my words can either nor my pen express ... I stood and gazed and gazed again at the exceeding loveliness before me as if I would make it part of my own soul ..."

The business part of the journey he faithfully pursued, finding Shetland herring much sought after and personal contacts with the Irish merchants productive. Some of them in Dublin and Waterford were not very impressed by the Shetland firm Hay & Ogilvy and disposed to deal with him instead. His return trip via the ferry to Holyhead allowed him to view the new industrial landscape of north England where he travelled on the Manchester railway and visited the silk mill of Royal and Crampton, the biggest in England, and Fawcett's iron foundry in Liverpool, employing at its height 700 men. There were Shetlanders here to offer hospitality – the Petister Hendersons took him to a concert by the violin vituoso Paganini, and their cousin, a serving soldier, showed him round the garrison castle of Chester.

The journal reveals a sensitive young man, who noticed people, their differences and their difficulties, and with a romantic susceptibility to beauty both natural and human: "I feel a strange disposition to fall in love with every girl I meet." Some of his female acquaintances were by no means unresponsive to such a sympathetic interlocutor, but although William naturally found this flattering he was not thereby rendered undiscriminating, and was aware when more worldly motives intruded, such as Mr Henderson's "great idea of uncle's wealth" which might, he thought, have influenced his daughter's behaviour. In any case William read her easily: "of one thing I am sure Miss H would not be happy in Shetland".

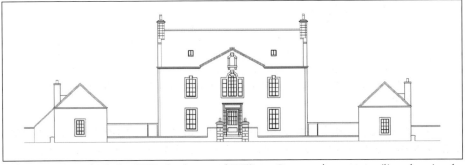

Belmont House, built in 1775, the home of William Cameron's parents. (line drawing by Mike Finnie for the Belmont Trust).

He enjoyed his trip, but felt the lack of a companion with whom to share it, and his thoughts often turned homewards. The back of his notebook filled up with a list of improvements for the family home at Belmont, and by the summer of 1832 he was back in Unst getting some of them under way against the return of his parents from a visit south. He wrote to lighten their enforced delay, shipbound on the *Magnus Troil* in Bressay Sound due to a cholera scare. "The ponies are in very good condition and you will be able to get some good of them ... there is every prospect of abundance of corn and grass this season and much need there is after last season's short crop ..."

But this optimistic assessment was to be proved wrong. Only two days later Shetland experienced the kind of summer storm which, unheralded and unexpected, has so often wreaked havoc by land and sea. On 19th July 1832, he wrote again to his parents in more sombre vein:

> Last Monday was a sad night here. Of 12 Unst boats only one got back to Unst and two reached Fetlar. Of the remaining nine no tidings are or can be expected for as the winds were unless they got to Skerries they must have all perished. At one time eight boats were seen to the lee of the Hill of Haroldswick but were gradually swept away and only one of them reached Fetlar. One boat was so near Lambaness that the people on shore could see the fish and other things on the boat but yet were swept away – but afterwards got to Fetlar. Six Fetlar and seven East Yell boats 22 in all are missing. The most of my boats were out with their nets and got safe back except one Magnus Thomason from Muness who went to the haaf and for whom I am afraid there is little hope. All here are sadly down about it – and no wonder.

Four years later, in January 1836, William Mouat of Garth and Annsbrae died unexpectedly at Geneva, during an extended trip abroad. His settlements were not as expected. Mouat had done his best to disinherit his nephew. He could not alter the succession of the Garth Estate, which went to his half-sister Margaret Cameron under the terms of Thomas Mouat's will, but he burdened it with all his outstanding liabilities. His other possessions – the Annsbrae lands which had come to him from his father, his valuable library, and Gardie House and its contents – were liferented to his wife, to come to William Cameron after her death. "By these arrangements," Mouat had written, "William Cameron has nothing from me but his stock in trade at Uyeasound."

Thus young William, far from taking control of his own destiny, found himself "without a shilling that at present I can say is my own". In addition, the revelation of his uncle's behaviour and real feelings towards him, after years of seeming confidence, must have been personally hurtful, for duplicity was foreign to young William's own nature. The situation now involved his parents, entirely unversed in estate management, and hitherto so far removed from Shetland business that they had no idea even of the rental of the Garth Estate. It complicated matters further that the widowed Eliza Mouat – a person of "naturally high temperament, rendered more so by excessive indulgence"[11] – suspected everyone including her hitherto loved nephew of colluding to cheat her, and her hysterical and demanding behaviour was a further burden on William, who stayed with her at Gardie and found himself de facto in charge of affairs. He found himself coping with difficult people and situations and a new order of things, though his affection for Gardie House, which had become his home, remained unchanged. "It is with so much happiness that I find myself again at home, tho' this house be very different indeed from what it has been in former days ..." William wrote his mother that October.

In this situation the Edinburgh lawyer John Phin was to assume a pivotal role. Phin's professional reputation was high – he was no stranger to the Westminster corridors of power – and to a cool and lucid brain he allied personal integrity. He had acted for William Mouat for several years and was therefore already familiar with at least some of the parameters of the situation; he was also

A line drawing, with colour wash, of William Mouat Cameron Mouat (he assumed the surname Mouat after the death of his uncle).

on terms of personal friendliness with the beleaguered William Cameron. He now accepted Captain and Mrs Cameron as clients. As for Eliza Mouat, she was persuaded to take independent legal advice to forestall accusations of partiality and, as Phin must have judged probable, was duly advised to renounce her life interest in Bressay and Noss, accept the alternative of a guaranteed annuity, and shake the dust of Shetland from her feet.

The way now became clearer for the Cameron parents to ascertain just what kind of situation they now confronted. They had inherited very heavy debts, something profoundly unacceptable to them both; almost their first act was to use the money which had come to Mrs Cameron from her mother's family to pay off the £2500 debt to the National Bank of Scotland. That there were many more liabilities was clear. Captain Cameron's disgust and anger at his late brother-in-law fuelled some outspoken letters to Phin, but the Captain, having vented his feelings, turned his energies to an attempt to improve the situation, and was quick to recognise the steady judgement that underpinned Phin's moderating letters.

Phin considered that the key to recovery lay in the person of the young William Cameron, now aged 26. "I am exceedingly anxious," he wrote, "that he should ... feel his own interest so completely identified with Zetland as to induce him to endeavour to gain the sympathies and confidence of the inhabitants of all ranks ... in Zetland he may be great, and do much good ..."

This assessment was shared by Captain and Mrs Cameron, whose letters to their son during those tense months were uniformly positive and supportive, whatever the feelings expressed elsewhere. William himself, initially naturally disappointed at his uncle's will, put such feelings behind him, having worked out a fallback position for himself: should things not work out for him in Shetland, he would emigrate. Agreement with his parents, however, was quickly reached. They continued to live in Unst and now formally appointed William factor for the Garth Estate, thus not only stabilising his position but utilising the knowledge and experience acquired over the past few years. This act of faith, after the blows of the preceeding few months, was personally reassuring to William, although he recognised what it would involve. On the evening of his 27th birthday William wrote his mother from Gardie:

... now I have a great and deep responsibility upon my shoulders – the comfort and the happiness of more than two thousand of my fellow creatures, your trust has confided to my care, a charge for which ... I pray for the means to be afforded me of doing my duty as I ought ... I deeply feel the responsibility I am under, but conscious and happy in that consciousness that will rather attribute to want of knowledge or experience, rather than to want of will where I go astray. (29 July 1837).

But life was not to deal William many easy cards. His assumption of responsibility coincided with a time of great difficulty in Shetland. Bad weather in the years after 1835 saw a series of failures in harvests and the eclipse of both the cod and herring fisheries, a state of affairs precipitating a widespread collapse in confidence. His father described the autumn of 1836 to the lawyer John Phin:

Such a melancholy harvest has not been witnessed in these islands by its oldest inhabitants ... a constant succession of rain and gales of wind ... much of the crop still green and uncut and what is cut down lying out in the fields ...

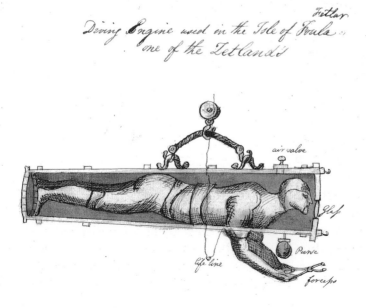

"Diving engine used in the isle of Foula (Fetlar), one of the Zetlands."

Business failure followed personal calamity. The closure of the Shetland branch of the National Bank of Scotland in 1838 was to be a precurser to the failure of the Shetland Bank and its parent company Hay & Ogilvie in 1842.[12] The effects were quickly apparent. "The prospect," William had written in October 1836, "is really very gloomy. Last year bad, my means and credit stretched to procure a subsistence for the people, of which I fear a large part from the bad fishing will never be repaid me, which of course not only hurts me, but takes away the means of helping the people again out of my hands ..." He was additionally faced with the plight of those "saving people" who had given their money for safekeeping into the hands of William Mouat:

> ... it bears peculiarly hard upon them that in a season like the present of extreme distress, they cannot command their hardwon store. Several individuals I have advanced sums to, upon my own account, but of course nothing to the extent that would be required.

William was now living alone at Gardie House. His aunt had taken much of the furniture to Edinburgh; the house around him was dark and silent. He lived in one room, with Jean Henderson, now the only house servant remaining at the house, to look after him. He was too much alone, oppressed by the knowledge of distress that he was powerless to alleviate and with the constant threat of bankruptcy hanging over him. William Mouat had been a guarantor for the debts of the banking speculator Yorstan; the unscrupulous dealings of the Belfast fish merchant Hannan proved equally impossible to settle.

Phin's advice was stringent – under no circumstances was there to be any borrowing of money. William's only alternative therefore was to sell. Even this was far from easy. He was forced to sell Garthspool, having unsuccessfully advertised for a tenant not only locally but in Wick, Peterhead and Aberdeen. He himself considered that the difficulty was "the want of capital to carry on a trade ... there are none who have the means and the will in [Shetland]". He had no alternative but to carry grimly on, unhappy with his "present unsettled factorship life" ("I have been at a public meeting this day for 6 mortal hours") knowing that the situation was not amenable to rapid resolution, lonely, and knowing he could not afford to marry. He could not discuss matters fully with his parents whose understanding was inevitably limited and who were in any case interested parties in the situation. His only confidant was John Phin, by letter.

Over the next two years William struggled to continue, selling land and assets to pay off debts, bitterly aware of the depressed conditions around him. His parents were anxious at the constant strain on him. They therefore took the chance, in the summer of 1838, to get William temporarily away from Shetland. Their youngest child, their son Thomas, was about to leave for India, destined for an army career. Captain and Mrs Cameron declared themselves unable for health reasons to travel to London to see him off; instead, they sent William and his sister Annie. So it was that William found himself at the London docks, saying goodbye to his brother. India had made the fortune of many a young hopeful; it had killed many more. It must have crossed William's mind that this might be a final parting; so indeed it was to prove. But perhaps upper-most in William's mind, as he turned his face once more to the north, was the contrast between the adventurous life opening up to his brother, and his own thankless exis-tence. Such feelings were reinforced on arrival in Edin-burgh to find his sister Jane engaged to marry one of the Dumfriesshire cousins. William, typical brother, was astonished by the news – though pleased too – but it seems that he now decided that his solitary life was no longer acceptable.

It was in this frame of mind that, at the time of Jane's wedding, he himself became engaged to Sarah

Coulson. Her widowed mother "to my surprise knew almost as much about Shetland as I did, having in her early days known a Miss Cumming who had been at Simbister". When William came home that autumn it was, for the first time for a long time, with hope. His parents were delighted. "We are now on a visit to William," wrote his father from Bressay that September, "who is busy getting this old house more comfortable than it has been for some while back, and when he has got the house properly repaired I hope he will take to himself a helpmeet."

But the hopes of happiness entertained by William were to be most cruelly shattered. Mrs Coulson had expectations of a financial settlement on her daughter far in excess of what the estate, debt and poverty ridden, could possibly provide, and in spite of William undertaking a desperate trip to Edinburgh in November 1838 in an attempt to reach agreement, the lady saw fit to break the engagement definitively by letter in early December. Miss Coulson's feelings are not recorded. William Cameron was alone in Gardie when the letter came.

He later confessed to his father:

> ... it has made me quite wretched since I got the letter. I have really since my uncle's death had so much to harass and annoy me, and with such a miserable state of the country for the last three years, that to have my hopes for something more like quietness and happiness than I have had for some time past, overset and dissipated, would have been the crowning stroke of the whole, and for the time at least too much for me.

William spent Christmas at home with his family at Belmont, making a gallant attempt to conceal his unhappiness. By January he was at Uyeasound, where at Gardiesfauld he received yet another demand for repayment of one of his uncle's debts. "if I must pay it, the sooner the better," he commented grimly. The pressure of work did not let up. "I have just finished half a quire in letters since I began today," wrote William to Phin. But the strain finally proved too much. In January William was taken ill at Gardiesfauld, and his father, having ridden over to see him, acted with characteristic briskness – "nothing like checking disease if possible at the commencement" – and had him brought to Belmont so that he could be nursed at home. Captain Cameron then rode north to see Dr Edmondston, who came to Belmont the following day, and from then on, troubled by the extent of William's collapse, the doctor remained in nearly constant attendance, sitting with him all night with the nurse.

Some five weeks later William had rallied enough to dictate to his sister Elizabeth a letter to Phin in which he described himself as having "not the strength of a straw", but as it was to prove, mind and body had been tested beyond the possibility of recovery. On 8th April he suffered a "severe paralytic attack ... which also deprived him of the power of speech". He lingered thus for a week before slipping away "in the arms of his devotedly attached mother", his family around him with Drs Edmondston and Spence, who had arrived that morning from Lerwick, and his "most attentive and assiduous sick nurse".

Dr Edmondston considered that death had resulted from the over-exertion and anxiety caused by the cumulative difficulties of the past three years – "the harassments and annoyances proceeding from Hannan's herring concerns and the complicated concerns of Yorston's banking speculations, along with the miserable poverty of the tenants", and finally, the last straw in Captain Cameron's opinion, the wrecked hopes of personal happiness conveyed by Mrs Coulson's letter breaking his engagement.

William was buried at Lund in Unst, in the quiet graveyard on the shores of the island that he loved. The funeral attracted large numbers of mourners: "no death" wrote his father, "has occurred in this country for many years that has been so universally deeply regretted." And they were right to grieve. The loss, most acute for his family, was to bear a bitter harvest in years to come. In the meantime Captain and Mrs Cameron, staggering under the weight of a personal agony better left unimagined, were faced with a crisis which affected not only themselves but all the people on the lands of Garth and Annsbrae.

NOTES:

1   GHA 2225/1815.

2   Thomas Mouat had built Belmont House in 1775; his brother John the smaller Annsbrae in Lerwick in 1791. Both are Georgian in style, accomplished in execution, and differ in both conception and mindset from the haa houses which were the norm.

3   Martha Gillie's father George was a blacksmith from the Borders, one of the many skilled Scotsmen who came to Shetland. It is possible that Gillie came at the instigation of the Shetland Society. He lived in the south end of Lerwick where Gillie's Pier is named after him (Thomas Manson, *Lerwick During the Last Half-century 1867-1917*).

4   Walking long distances across the hill to work was not uncommon and long persisted. The late Peter Manson of Mizpah, Bressay, started work in 1930 aged 14, walking daily from his home at the Maryfield farm steading to Bruntland, Aith – almost exactly the same route as William Edgar, but in reverse.

5   *Sons and Daughters of Shetland 1800-1900*, Margaret Stuart Robertson.

6   Two contemporaries of William Mouat's, both members of the Edmondstone family, had children by their housekeepers.

7   *Shetland Miscellany* Vol 9.

8   Garthspool, built by John Mouat in 1822.

9   Hay's Dock, adjacent to Garthspool.

10   After the rising of United Irishmen under Wolfe Tone in 1798 the British government passed the Act of Union whereby in January 1801 Ireland became part of the United Kingdom.

11   Captain Cameron to John Phin, October 1836.

12   Hance Smith, *Shetland Life and Trade*.

CHAPTER FIVE

CAPTAIN CAMERON MOUAT

> *The poverty and distress prevailing in the islands for these*
> *several years have rendered it impracticable to recover*
> *money ... in such circumstances it was deemed advisable*
> *(and has been found advantageous) rather to bear with*
> *the debtors, taking what could be got from time to time,*
> *than to expose their difficulties and ruin their credit ...*
> Gilbert Duncan, writer, Lerwick, to John Phin, writer, Edinburgh, October 1839.

Two days after the funeral of his son, Captain William Cameron, writing from a grief-stricken family home in Unst, described to his agent in Edinburgh how he had found himself "under the painful necessity of giving directions about shipping herrings for Mr Goddard etc while my dear son was yet a corpse in the house". Thus abruptly did the day-to-day responsibilities of estate management devolve on one who had never expected to have to assume them. "God's will be done;" he wrote, "and as we have endeavoured to discharge our duty to the dead, we must now endeavour to attend to the claims of the living."

In these terms William Cameron faced the situation that now confronted him. The reference to God bespeaks a bereaved parent attempting to come to terms with an agonising loss; but "duty" and the necessity of practicality were all his own traits, deeply ingrained by the circumstances of his own life. William Cameron's own family had been refugees, displaced in the violent aftermath of the 1745 Jacobite

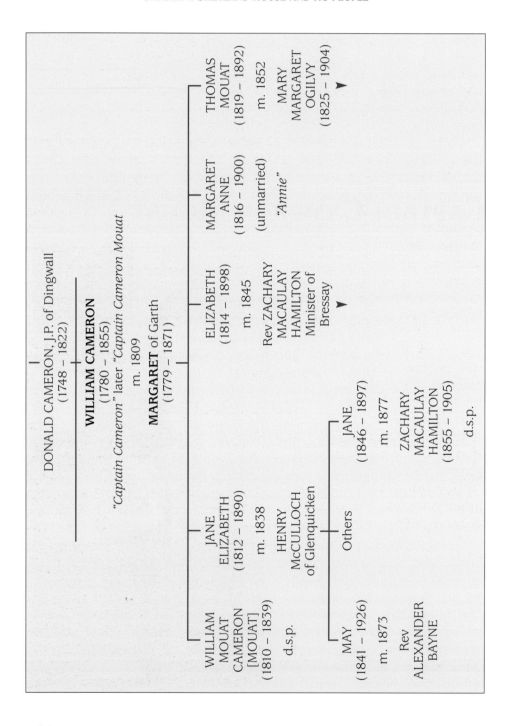

DONALD CAMERON, J.P. of Dingwall
(1748 – 1822)

WILLIAM CAMERON
(1780 – 1855)
"Captain Cameron" later "Captain Cameron Mouat
m. 1809
MARGARET of Garth
(1779 – 1871)

WILLIAM
MOUAT
CAMERON
[MOUAT]
(1810 – 1839)
d.s.p.

JANE
ELIZABETH
(1812 – 1890)
m. 1838
HENRY
McCULLOCH
of Glenquicken

ELIZABETH
(1814 – 1898)
m. 1845
Rev ZACHARY
MACAULAY
HAMILTON
Minister of
Bressay ▶

MARGARET
ANNE
(1816 – 1900)
(unmarried)
"Annie"

THOMAS
MOUAT
(1819 – 1892)
m. 1852
MARY
MARGARET
OGILVY
(1825 – 1904) ▶

MAY
(1841 – 1926)
m. 1873
Rev
ALEXANDER
BAYNE

JANE
(1846 – 1897)
m. 1877
ZACHARY
MACAULAY
HAMILTON
(1855 – 1905)
d.s.p.

Others

rebellion. They changed their name and gained a farm tenancy at Rosskeen, on the shores of the Cromarty Firth. Two generations later it was safe to call yourself "Cameron" again, and William's father Donald had entered the professional classes as a writer in Dingwall and J.P. for Ross and Cromarty. Without land, money or connections, however, the boys had to make their own way in the world.

War provided an opportunity. William, the eldest son, was the first of the six brothers to enter the service of the British crown. One died a midshipman in Java; but the others entered the army, and all survived the French wars which lasted from 1792 until final victory at Waterloo in 1815. William Cameron himself, a lieutenant in the 78th Highlanders, served in Sicily and Italy, and commanded a company at the battle of

Maida[1] where his young soldiers, "opposing and conquering a veteran enemy", were commended for their "courage, spirit, and steady conduct".[2] Afterwards he served in Egypt, where he was on the staff of General MacKenzie Fraser, and where his brother officers valued him sufficiently to present him with a silver gilt cup "as a mark of their personal regard" and as thanks for his "unremitting and zealous attention to ... the interior economy of the regiment".[3]

Lieutenant Cameron's uniform and other mementoes, exhibited in the Regimental museum at Fort George.

When the Regiment returned to Britain, Lieutenant Cameron was sent on a recruiting trip to Shetland, and it was then that he met and won his lady – Margaret Mouat, the niece of Thomas Mouat, who with his wife Elizabeth had raised her at Belmont. The marriage proved a supremely happy one. The Camerons spent the rest of the war years in Aberdeen, where Captain Cameron commanded the regimental depot, but after a severe attack of rheumatic fever in 1815, which he survived in spite of all that medical science could do – he was blooded eight times – he retired on half pay. The Camerons came back to Shetland and settled at Belmont, which became theirs after Thomas Mouat's death in 1819. There they raised a family of five children, living a quiet life removed in both style and substance from William Mouat and the high profile high spend regime at Gardie House.

It was not until William Mouat's unexpected death in 1836 that the Cameron parents became aware of the situation bequeathed them, and their dismay is well documented by Captain Cameron's letters to John Phin, the Edinburgh lawyer who was to play a significant role in future events. The Camerons had asked their elder son William to run the Garth estate on their behalf, and the Annsbrae estate for his aunt Eliza, now living in Edinburgh. Their younger son Thomas had recently commenced his career in India, in the army of the East India Company. After William's death in 1839 his parents wrote immediately with the grim news, and a plea for Tom's return, but in the inevitable interregnum, there was no alternative but that Captain Cameron, now aged 55, should take over the administration of a large landed estate.

Captain Cameron cannot have been other than well aware of the nature of the burden he now shouldered. It had killed his son. Shetland remained economically primitive: wedded to the chancy performance of the fishings, coupled with a backward agriculture and at the mercy of the weather for both. Viewed from a distance, the islands did not perform well; not without reason did the cool-headed Phin, the family's agent in Edinburgh and intimately acquainted with Shetland business for more than a decade, advise the youthful Thomas Cameron to be wary of abandoning his profession to return to the islands.

As Captain Cameron examined the state of affairs of the landed property now to be dealt with himself – the Lerwick writer Gilbert Duncan found him "minutely particular" in business affairs (May 1839) – he found a situation where a succession of "bad crops and indifferent fishings" rendered the estate income ill-prepared to fund the public and private burdens it faced. By 1840 land was assessed for the provision of public services, and the monies due were of course paid out of estate revenue i.e. rents.[4] By 1851 these liabilities were calculated at 10/8½ d in £1, or over half the rental value.

Landowning was becoming uneconomic, a state of affairs which would lead proprietors to examine how the land was used and managed. Elsewhere agricultural improvement, necessary to feed a growing population, also implied money rents, and evictions from uneconomic holdings. Not however that these remedies suggested themselves to Captain Cameron Mouat. Unversed in either the theory or practice of landowning, his instinct was to keep going and hope for the best. "By the time all the sums are paid," he wrote his brother Alexander in September 1839, "there will remain but a small surplus for ourselves, so much for the name of a large estate in these poor islands – we hope however for a better time when a gracious Providence sees proper to give us good crops and better fishings – but till then we must struggle on the best we can."

His own and his wife's horror of debt resulted in a calling in of sums owed and a paying of those left unpaid as far as could be managed; his ledgers record the setting straight of affairs wherever possible; but these were almost entirely small sums. The heavy debts incurred by William Mouat on the security of Garth, which included a heritable Bond for £5000, were and remained beyond the capability of the estate to pay off, and finding the interest payable, in addition to the large annuity due twice yearly to Eliza Mouat in Edinburgh, was to be a constant battle.

Once it was clear that Thomas was not coming back (his superior officers refused him special leave of absence), Captain and Mrs Cameron set themselves to a radical change in their lives. They decided to assume the surname Mouat, an example followed by their two unmarried daughters, Anne and Elizabeth. (From India their son Thomas, declining to follow suit, commented: "I must say I like Cameron better.") The family began to live at Gardie House for extended periods, tending to be in Unst for the summer months and Bressay through the winter. There, after Elizabeth's marriage to the Rev Zachary Macaulay Hamilton[5], minister of Bressay, in 1845, a clutch of children, Elizabeth's stepchildren from Mr Hamilton's first marriage and then her own babies, brought laughter into their lives again.

Drawing of Belmont House showing the farm buildings and parks.

A family man, loved by his children and grandchildren and tenacious of his friends[6] – it was a good base from which to face difficulties, but Captain Cameron Mouat had more than that to sustain him. To an unfamiliar job he brought his own particular strengths. He had lived in Unst for twenty years and known Shetland for thirty; he was a good judge of people, robustly sensible, and possessed, saving grace par excellence, a sense of humour. Having learned in the Army that a good officer knows his men, he applied this principle to estate management; and in his notes and ledgers he wrote down not only what he had done, but why, and very often a comment on the person involved. (He was right to think that knowing people and their circumstances assisted decision-making; later on Charles Gilbert Duncan, who was to become factor for the Annsbrae estate, commented on the difficulties he encountered during his first year in post "from my unacquaintance with the people and ignorance of the actual state of their means and substance" (October 1852).

Estate income derived from the land. During the first decades of the 19th century the old system of fishing tenures fell into disuse, as landowners increasingly realised the advantages of money rents. In

Bressay about two-thirds of his tenants still fished to William Mouat in 1821; fifteen years later, the rental of 1838 shows exclusively money rents. Fishing was now the province of merchants, but irrespective of however it was organised and by whom the risks and uncertainties remained. Hay & Ogilvie, who rented the herring station at Hogan in Bressay for a rent of 6d per cran of herrings cured, saw their throughput plummet to a mere 179 ½ crans in 1841, recorded "by their Cooper's return". The rent due came to £4/9/9d.

In the north of Shetland records show that it was much harder to move to money rents – perhaps due to local conservatism; that this was not at all the wish of Captain Cameron Mouat is borne out by his comment to John Phin in November 1839:

> ... there is very little profit to be derived from the fishings, the great good of them is to have the rents better paid. I should not regret if the old boats, old lines and old nets were along with the fish at the bottom of the sea; there is nothing but annoyance and vexation, and I shall rejoice when I am free of these fishing concerns.

Unfortunately this was easier said than done. Initially Hay & Ogilvy took over the whole complicated business for the estate in the North Isles. After the collapse of the firm in 1842 Charles Ogilvy himself briefly took on the task, but after that Captain Cameron Mouat had to do it himself, and organise local men to ship the fish. It never appealed to him, and he had a low opinion of the whole set-up, especially the calibre of local fishcurers and traders: " you know what they are" he commented to Charles Gilbert Duncan in 1850.

It is clear that the old system was breaking down. On the Garth lands Captain Cameron Mouat set the price of the fish, but such was the passive resistance that he had to pay a bounty plus premiums to the first two boats. The estate was no longer making fishing a condition of letting farms, and indeed, Captain Cameron Mouat himself had different priorities.

In February 1855 George Henderson of Burravoe in Yell, finding the difficulties of manning his Unst boats becoming endemic, tried to lease the touns of Houlland and Woodwick in west Unst from the Captain with the explanation: "my few tenants in Petister fishes to me at Woodwick; generally they do get free men in Unst to fill up the boats and sometimes are obliged to get a few even from Yell for that purpose."

Captain Cameron Mouat, however, refused: "while the present tenants paid their rents they (will) not be removed by me".

Other problems were described by Gilbert Gauden, estate factor in Unst:

> ...on account of Andrew Edwardson's removal from Collaster, that boat has been nearly broken up for want of a skipper, and no such man to be got; I at last prevailed with the Houlnon men to spare Magnus Edwardson. I have however got a lad to go in the Houlnon boat, but he is one of the volunteers likely to be called out in May ...

If it was a question of new boats the crew, not unreasonably, expected to get what they wanted: when Peter Hunter of Noustigarth in Bressay was employed by the estate to build a boat for the Houlnon men in Unst, many an anxious note went to and fro. It wore Captain Cameron Mouat to a frazzle (though by then it is true he was sick and failing). The dysfunctionality of such a non-money economy in a changing world was apparent – change could not be avoided, although it might be postponed.

Money rents had another advantage, as must have quickly become clear. They could be altered. Captain Cameron Mouat's detailed accounts, heavily annotated, show his frequent habit of discounting rents in response to cases of hardship. Donald Winwick in Muness, Unst was discounted £2.12.6d "on account of the state of his family" in the rent account for 1855. Bereavement discounts were so frequent that the widows' names are not given; and bad harvests were also a common cause, like the Haraldswick tenants in the late 1840s.

Thomas Penney, who held the farms of Keldabister and Cruister in Bressay at half-yearly rents of £26 and £10 respectively, was discounted £5 in 1846 and £7 the following year when his potato crop was a nearly total failure. John Ward, tenant of Garth and Culbinsbrough, was advanced a cash loan of 10/- in 1844 as he was going south. He was later alleged to have "died abroad in 1846" but as Captain Cameron Mouat noted, underlined, this was "not believed"! At the same reckoning Ward's neighbour John Halcow was penalised, at the moderate amount of 6d, for "cutting feals in Ander Hill".

The mainstay of the estate was the large number of small farms, tenanted at the pleasure of the landowner, theoretically annually. Records show that many farms remained in the same family for substantial periods of time and Captain Cameron Mouat and his factor

Gilbert Gauden in South Unst shared the same emphatic desire for stability – "I am quite of your opinion as to the evil of shifting tenants," as Captain Cameron Mouat commented. When people did try to move, Captain Cameron Mouat discouraged them if he could. Age or ill health often seems to have been a factor, not surprising when one considers the physical demands of unmechanised farming. Matthew Ogilvy wanted to give up his holding of Framgord for which he had a three-year lease because of ill health, and when James Sharp wanted to move from Muness to Littlagarth he was told he would lose his 30/- annual wage as ground officer. He decided not to go, but negotiated through Gilbert Gauden a reduction of rent and of the size of his present farm.

Nonetheless the rural situation was by now inherently unsustainable. Land hunger was a feature especially in those parts of the estate where there were no alternatives to farming. The failed sheep farm at Lumbister in North Yell was once again populated; the estate built new houses there in 1852. At the 1861 census three houses contained a total population of thirty-one persons[7], in conditions, it may be conjectured, of overcrowding, poor sanitation, and little access to education for any children; a recipe, in fact, for the perpetuation of poverty and the encouragement of tuberculosis, which flourished in such conditions. Rent arrears were common – in 1851 the North Yell tenants were nearly all two years in arrear, and some three years, and the total cash take was £1.4.6d – but there was no suggestion of eviction.

That Captain Cameron Mouat was well known to his tenants is evident from their readiness to approach him personally. In April 1855, Andrew Thompson, who had tenanted six merks of land at Setter in Unst for twenty-five years, wrote Captain Cameron Mouat:

> I have been a widower for more than 24 years and I have 2 sons that were born lame, they are all of my own family that now remains with me; they are so very lame both in hands and feet that they can do nothing for themselves. The oldest one is more than 30 years old ... I can no longer keep a farm, I am truly at a loss what to think about my two sons. I might find lodgings for myself with some relation but alas I have no relation who can take them and although they are lame they are very dear to me, nor can I bear the idea of them being laid on the Parish while I am able to do anything for them. I therefore beg to ask if you will allow me to put up a small house outside and near the Hill Dike of Setter where it can come least in the way of the tenants ...

Captain Cameron Mouat's distinctive signature.

Captain Cameron Mouat, despite believing that Thompson was "doing wrong in giving up his farm in Setter", agreed to this, giving him also peat rights and a small piece of ground for a kail yard, and got Laurence Sinclair of Skea to look over the ground for a suitable site out of the way of the Setter tenants' cattle going to pasture. The Captain, having considered further, then wrote Thompson that "if the neighbouring tenants do not object to (you) having a cow, a horse and some sheep grazing in the scattald while it remains underused, I shall not object". In the event Andrew Thompson decided to stay put for another year anyway and "to give timely notice of removal".

The estate wanted, and needed, good tenants, and when it had them, wanted to keep them.

In July 1851 James Thomason and his wife Jacobina Wynwick were offered a life rent extending to second death of their farm of eight merks of land at Noustigarth in Muness "with all parts, pertinents and privileges belonging to the same as presently occupied by you, at the yearly rent of six pounds sterling", without a condition of fishing but with stipulations about land use:

> ... your peat ground to continue as it has been for the last five years. You are not to encroach on any of your neighbours' peat grounds, and whenever you cut peats the upper sod must be carefully laid down with the grass side uppermost. You are not to subset or assign any part of your farm to any person whatever, you are to keep good neighbourhood, and prevent your animals from trespassing upon any of your

neighbours' grounds; if you keep any swine they must be kept tied in a yard, or in some small enclosure by themselves, or with a sufficiently strong ring in the snout of each swine so as to prevent completely their turning up the soil or grass with their snouts.

You are not to cut any feals or spade peats within your Town dykes, but in the proper places set apart for that purpose. In the event of your being employed or engaged in the salvage or driving of any whales you shall be bound to account to me for the ground share of said whales received by you, being a third part of the whales so salved by you.

You are not to keep a shop, or sell spirits of any description, or purchase, or receive in way of barter, any fish from neighbouring tenant ... You will forfeit this lease of tack if you allow the rent to run in arrear for a larger sum than six pounds sterling.

Wishing you and your wife health and long life to enjoy your lease ...

The inevitable disputes could have their funny side. In February 1854 the "serious injury to pasture and corn" caused by geese resulted in a blanket ban being imposed on the keeping of geese in Bressay. "No exception can be allowed," wrote Captain Cameron Mouat, "seeing that any favour to one tenant would be acting unjustly to his neighbours – 'Sauce for a goose must be sauce for a gander.'"

There were quarrels about stock going over dykes and the owner's refusal to accept responsibility. One such was Thomas Sutherland of Hogaland in Unst, "an obstinate, witless body" according to Joseph Leisk of Uyea, describing how Sutherland's almark[8] horses drove in the dyke at Mula and destroyed the hay park, "all we had to depend on to save the cattle in the spring". In fact the toun dyke was too low. "I have known cows go over it in the summer season some years ago," remarked Gilbert Gauden.

Another dyke, the division dyke between Ramnageo and Scollay in south Unst, took more than a year to be built up: "the Ramnageo tenants built their share of it last spring," wrote John Mouat, wright, as a footnote to his bill to Capt Cameron Mouat for harling Gardies Fauld at Uyeasound and work at Belmont making doors and skylights for the Farmer's House, "but the Scollay and Noustigarth tenants do not seem disposed to do so and these tenants make a regular pasture of Ramnageo ..."

It was not uncommon for groups of tenants, exasperated by bad neighbours and crop losses, to ask the estate to build proper dykes; they too saw the advantages of enclosure. The farm at Braehead, at Norwick

Bressay women taking their produce to Lerwick by boat. On this occasion the cargo includes geese. © *Shetland Museum*

in the north of Unst, was not the only one to be "rendered much more productive by being properly enclosed", as was noted in 1840. The standard arrangement was that tenants paid 7½ % interest on the cost of building, but the building itself provided work, as did a modest programme of road building. In Bressay John Edgar, the farmer at Setter, was paid from 1840 onwards as overseer or superintendent of the roadmen.

The tenants of small farms had another incentive to enclose – the ready market which was now emerging for their cattle. Improved techniques on the bigger farms – the use of turnips for winter feed and better grassland management of the newly laid out parks – meant that they could support more cows than formerly. Competition for young beasts could be lively.

The home farm at Belmont looked for no fewer than 30 in the spring of 1855, but demand, as often happened, outstripped supply:

> I have all along made a point of not interfering with the tenants' cattle
> further than to see that they paid the value to rent account and they
> have consequently had liberty to sell to any person who would give the
> highest price... most farrow cows have either been sold or promised ...

wrote Charles Gilbert Duncan that April when enquiries, unsuccessful in Unst, spread to Yell.

Estate finances, as will be apparent, were not sound in terms of rental income, especially given the hands-on, idiosyncratic management style; and expenditure remained high with a constant if small programme of infrastructural improvement. The whole remained viable because both Captain and Mrs Cameron Mouat inherited some money from their Scottish families, and used it to underpin estate finances; and because for several years there was a good income from chromate in Unst, and the slate quarries in Bressay. It was possible to keep things going, but there was no extra money, mercifully, to fund the kind of grandiloquent "improvements" to either Gardie House or Belmont which ruined so many traditional haa houses.

Captain and Mrs Cameron Mouat, with a mindset traditional, personal and Christian, tried to do the best they could for the people. They were known for their punctilious payment of Poor Relief dues[9] – which must have been a relief to the Rev Barclay, who, newly appointed Collector of Poor Rates in Yell, in May 1851 asked particularly for prompt payment due on estate lands in Yell "as our Parochial Board is just now entirely without funds". [10]

In 1851 Captain Cameron Mouat offered the Highland Relief Board a deal: he would build a pier or public landing place in Bressay costing up to £35 on condition that the Board expended three times that sum in giving employment to the destitute population in North Yell. In fact estate tenants – men and lasses – did work on the Cooperation Road from Cullivoe to Midyell with ½ of their wages going where appropriate to credit against unpaid rent, but they declined further employment on the Midyell to Burravoe road, presumably because of the distance involved.

Captain Cameron Mouat had earlier taken up the cudgels on behalf of whale salvers, when he became Convenor of the Commissioners of Supply.

One of his first acts was to write to the Shetland MP Frederick Dundas regarding the plight of the salvers of a large whale which came ashore at Outer Ska, Unst in August 1839:

> Mr Maconochie the Vice-Admiral of the county being then in Lerwick I lost no time in making a report to him on the subject, at the same time expressing a hope that this finner whale should be given up to the salvers (9 poor fishermen). Mr Maconochie kindly answered my letter at

the same time expressing his regret that he was obliged to claim all large whales as "Droits of Admiralty" and to account for their proceeds in Exchequer. I had consequently nothing further to urge on behalf of my poor tenants. This large and poor whale was soon after sold for £5 – which merely paid the 9 salvers 7/6d each, being at the rate of 1/6d per day for the 5 days and nights they were engaged in flenshing and watching the blubber of this whale, besides some small incidental expenses.

I trust this plain statement will show you the hardship to which our poor fishermen are subjected with regards to these large and poor whales ... and how very trifling, if any, are the benefits which Her Majesty's Exchequer is likely to derive from the occasional poor whale cast ashore on our islands.

Dundas required further prodding nearly a year later when some other fishermen were due to be prosecuted "for having at the risk of their lives salved a small portion of the blubber of a putrid whale." Captain Cameron Mouat suggested that as the Vice-Admiral had made a report proceedings should be held pending a decision from the lords of the Treasury. A month later judgement was duly handed down, a judgement thoroughly favourable to local feeling: although the Crown did not waive its rights, the Vice-Admiral was now empowered to use his discretion in remunerating salvers to a maximum of two-thirds of the proceeds, this ruling also to apply to small whales; and in the immediate case if judgement went against the fishermen they were to be recompensed.

Captain Cameron Mouat was also, by virtue of his landed estate, a heritor of Unst. This was to involve him in a lot of work. In the early 1840s a new manse was needed in the island after the minister, the Rev James Ingram, left his charge to become one of the Free Church clergy after the Disruption in the Church of Scotland[11]. The difficulty arose because Mr Ingram had used his own house as the manse (for which the Church of Scotland had paid him a yearly allowance of £27), and the incoming minister was therefore homeless. In the summer of 1844 the Rev Gordon McIntosh, now the Church of Scotland presence in Unst, wrote to Mr Stevenson, Moderator of the Burravoe Presbytery (whose remit extended to Unst), to ask that a suitable manse was built. The task – and the expense – fell to the Unst heritors.[12]

With the kind of dreadful inevitability which attends such decision-making, Captain Cameron Mouat found himself appointed by the usual committee to take charge of the whole process.

It proved to be an experience not without its moments. The initial stages of the project were distinguished by a succession of acrimonious arguments and accusations of bad faith, firstly about the survey of the site, then the design of the building, and finally about the appointment of the contractor. The good captain managed to avert a near disaster about the design of the manse, when the heritors, like gadarene swine, were seduced by the fancy of a double roof with a valley in between (the potential damage by heavy acumulations of snow in winter counting for less that the assertion that such a roof was cheaper than the alternative). Captain Cameron Mouat, with his usual practicality, visited Fort Charlotte in Lerwick and spent an afternoon climbing over the barracks roof with the men who maintained it, when he "saw enough and heard what was more than sufficient to convince me that the roof of your manse should not be a double roof".

Examples of skilled stonemasonry in Bressay and Lerwick.

Examples of skilled stonemasonry in Bressay and Lerwick.

To settle the strongly-expressed differences which characterise design by committee Captain Cameron Mouat suggested referring the plan to an Edinburgh architect, which gave everyone a convenient fall guy if required; but David Rhind, the architect thus appointed, made such unexceptional suggestions as adding servants' accommodation and porches, which "in such a climate I would consider almost essential to the comfort of the house"; and to assist the provision of internal warmth he suggested that the under part of the stair should be enclosed for a small wine and spirit cellar. It is not known how this suggestion was received by those of the heritors who, like the Rev Ingram, were strongly Temperance.

The contractor finally appointed was Joseph Leisk of Uya, farmer and house carpenter. Leisk was an able man and a good workman but he required firm handling – he promptly suggested, amongst other niggles, that a privy served just as well as a water closet "at one tenth of the expense", and at one point Captain Cameron Mouat had to get his Edinburgh lawyer to demolish Leisk's attempt to have the entire contract revised halfway through the project. But when it came to the actual building, Leisk delivered.

The detailed specification shows the kind of quality required:

> ... the back part of the lobby, the kitchen, the pantry, and kitchen closets to be laid with best Brassay (sic) flags, squared, close jointed, and not under two inches thick ... Easdale slates for the roof well bedded in plaster lime ... offices to consist of a byre and stable under one roof length 28 feet breadth 12 feet, a barn and milkhouse under one roof ... byre and stable floors to be partly causied and partly set with rough flags, milkhouse floor to be paved with smooth flags close jointed ... roofs to be covered with best Brassay slates that can be got ... timber in house to include Riga or Petersburgh deals and batons ... the inside finishing may be either of East Country timber or American yellow pine, free of sap wood, shakes or loose knots and properly seasoned. The whole of the work to be execute in the most substantial and workmanlike manner ...

James Laurenson, mason, of Deepdale, Dunrossness, was taken on as foreman at a salary of 20 shillings per week. By May 1847 the mason work was finished and drains installed in the house "for the outlet of water". Six months later Leisk was able to inform Captain Cameron Mouat that "the inside work is now going on apace. I am well pleased that

I got the manse and office houses roofed and closed in before the bad weather set in; I have not discovered any leaks in the roofs yet and I am hoping none will be."

The following summer the building was harled, and insured for £1110 for fire and other risks. It was formally inspected on behalf of the Burravoe Presbytery in December 1849 by William Halcrow, joiner in Lerwick, and James Laurenson, mason and inspector of works. The Presbytery declared themselves "fully satisfied with what has been done, with so much credit to the heritors themselves and so little trouble comparatively to the Presbytery ..." In thanking the committee, they mentioned particularly its "much respected convenor," Captain Cameron Mouat, "for the deep interest he has felt, and the great trouble he has taken in this and other matters connected with the welfare of the parish".

So Unst had its manse. Perhaps it is not surprising that in February 1849 the minister complained to Leisk about water at the windows but, as the latter commented:

> I am almost sure that there were few, if any, houses in Shetland that did not take in water on Tuesday the 30th of January last. The house of Uya took in water that day in places where no water had been seen for 30 years back; I am also sure that the manse of Unst is no worse than the generality of houses in Shetland and much better than most of them.

While the manse was building, Captain Cameron Mouat annotated one of the timber accounts with a shaky comment: "we may not all live to see the last payment". This was in 1847. In fact he lived another eight years, his health slowly declining, so that the once vigorous figure who rode and walked and spoke among the people became, eventually, housebound. This produced a mass of detailed correspondence, as he tried to keep abreast of events and problems as they arose.

He died in the summer of 1855 in Edinburgh, where he had gone to consult doctors, a tiny note sending his last message of love to his wife, at home in Shetland. His body was brought back to Unst for burial. His daughter Elizabeth, who had supervised the funeral arrangements on behalf of her mother, ran up to the top floor of Belmont House to watch as the cortege passed along the Loch of Snarravoe, up the brae to the shop at Garden, and on out of sight over the hilltop towards the church at Lund, where Captain Cameron Mouat lies beside his son William.

View from the rear of Belmont showing the route taken by Captain Cameron Mouat's funeral cortege in July 1855.

After Captain Cameron Mouat's death the estate was owned by his widow; but in fact the decision-making seems to have been undertaken largely by their daughter, Anne. Unfortunately Miss Mouat did not believe in keeping records, and the vivid picture of people and local happenings, so amply documented by her father and his correspondents, ends abruptly. The two ladies lived at Gardie House, awaiting the return of Thomas from India.

Major Thomas Cameron left Bombay for the last time in 1861, bringing home a trunk full of curios from the exotic East, and a personality shaped and warped by the experiences of his youth and adulthood. Service in India had meant long separation from his family – when he first went out in 1839 at the age of twenty, home leave was not allowed before eleven years service.

Cameron lacked influential friends, but did not die of disease or bullet and rose in rank to become Adjutant of the 55th Bengal Native

Light Infantry, one of the regiments which mutinied in 1857. The colonel, overcome with grief at the behaviour of men he had trusted, shot himself. Thomas Cameron himself acted with courage, and survived, as did his wife and two infant children[13]. In the reckoning which followed, one of his duties was to be present at executions.

These experiences must have taken their toll; but whatever the external influences it seems that he was anyway a cold and unsympathetic man. His letters to his parents show little interest in Shetland, nor even an attempt to understand the situation in which they found themselves, and were sometimes downright disparaging. "I have no doubt," he commented in 1848, "when I may be allowed to take any furlough I shall find Zetland pretty much as I fancy it to be, a pleasant residence for a few months in the year ..."

Without enthusiasm, therefore, Major Cameron returned to the islands of his birth. His family now comprised three children, a son William, a delicate, intelligent seven-year-old, born like his younger sister Jane in India, and a toddler, Peggy. After a brief stay at Gardie House with

A watercolour picture looking from the front gates of Gardie House towards Lerwick.

Major Cameron's mother and sister the family moved to Annsbrae House in Lerwick where they settled in 1863. Two children born there died in infancy.

Major Cameron had on his arrival in Shetland begun to familiarise himself with the state of the lands from which he was to make his living. He found much to disquiet him. National legislation was placing ever heavier public burdens upon land, as a means of financing local services, and the estate was additionally burdened with the debts left thirty years earlier by William Mouat.

Major Cameron had no private income to finance the improvements essential to generate income – his father had left what money there was to his sisters, the well meaning but disastrous act of a financial innocent. Such ventures as draining, fencing, farm roads, new houses – all had to be financed by estate income. Higher rents would only come from economic holdings; it was pointless to raise rents if tenants could not afford them, arrears were already a problem.

Greater prosperity, a better standard of living, money rents which tenants could pay – the need for all these things had been foreseen forty years previously by the Shetland Society. In the intervening years the Shetland population had soared to its highest recorded level (31,670 in the 1861 census).

Major Cameron had little personal interest in the people of Shetland and no understanding of their circumstances. He found the problems of running a landed estate both complicated and depressing – "each day is almost worse than its predecessor" – and, having no desire to tackle these problems himself, looked for someone to do the job for him. Immediately to his attention came an acquaintance recommended by the Rev Hamilton, a man who had recently taken over as tenant of Keldabister Farm in Bressay, one John Walker.

NOTES:

1   The battle of Maida, in July 1806, when a small British force under Sir John Stuart defeated a slightly larger French army commanded by Reynier. It was the only victory by British troops against French on the European mainland until Wellington's campaigns in the Peninsula, and many officers who later served under Wellington, including some who became household names, were present at Maida and witnessed the successful tactics employed.

2   Major-General David Stewart to Captain William Cameron, late of 78th Highland Regiment, October 1825.

3   The silver gilt cup, together with other relics of Captain Cameron's military career, may be seen in the Regimental Museum, Fort George, Inverness.

4   Services included teinds, land tax, rogue and prison money, building and repairing parish churches and parish schools, schoolmasters' salaries, assessments for the poor, building and repairing tenants' houses – Hance Smith p 127.

5   Zachary Macaulay Hamilton DD (1805-1876). Minister of Bressay from 1833; twice married and father of 10 children.

6   Sir Christian Ploien, Governor of Holbeck, Denmark, wrote Captain Cameron Mouat in August 1849 "you are the only man in Zetland who does not intirely blot me out of his memory, the connecting link between the islands and myself."

7   *Lonely, lovely Lumbister*, Robert L Johnson, Shetland Life Jan 1987.

8   Almark – an animal with no respect for boundaries.

9   Poor Law Minutes of Evidence 1843: "Mrs Mouat of Ansbray [sic] sent £5 in 1839, and £1 in 1842; and Captain Mouat sent likewise in the latter year £1. With these exceptions, we have not received a penny from any one of the non-resident heritors within my recollection ... Mrs Mouat sent her donation without any application being made to her ..." William Craigie, Session-Clerk of North Yell.

10 Poor Relief, which in any case was far from perfect; although the Scottish Poor Law had eventually been reformed in 1845, local parochial boards were slow to utilise the Act; it was only ten years later that the Bressay Parochial Board resolved to implement a legal assessment system at a rate of 6d per merk of land, to finance poor relief.

11 The Disruption of 1843, "the most momentous single event of the nineteenth century", when nearly 40% of the Church of Scotland's communicants withdrew, including more than 470 ministers out of 1200, raised questions not only about patronage, but more fundamentally about the place of the church in modern society and the constitution and powers of the state.

NOTES:

12   In 1845 the Unst heritors were – Captain Cameron Mouat, Thomas Edmondstone Esq of Buness, Rt Hon the Earl of Zetland, John Ogilvy Esq of Greenwall and Stove, William Leisk of Uya, Gilbert Spence Esq of Hammar, William Spence Esq of Greenfield, Mr William Henderson of Petister, Mr Charles Mouat of Brookpoint, Mr Andrew Spence of Westerhouse, Rev James Ingram of Hillside, Mr Nicol Henderson of Bodaw, Mr Magnus Fea of Clivocast, Mr Gilbert Smith of Smithfield, Mr James Spence of Houston, Mr Magnus Anderson of Houll, Mr Gilbert Gauden, Uyasound, Mr Charles Jamieson of Still, Mr John Jamieson of Still, Mr Charles Arthur of Bighton, Mr James Peterson – Peter Jamieson of Garrigarth, Mr David Nicolson of Lo Hammar, Mr James Jamieson of Greenroad.

13   Major Thomas Cameron married Mary Margaret Ogilvie, 1825-1904, daughter of John Ogilvie, M.D. of Boyndlie, Fraserburgh.

CHAPTER SIX

THE MAJOR AND HIS SISTER

*I have heard that you are removing the tenants of Logie
at Hallamas first. If so and no tenants entering into that
term, would you be good enough to allow the house to be
occupied by two of our paupers during the winter and spring
as they are dependent on the Parochial board for shelter and
nothing can be got up for them at this season of the year.*
William Pole, Greenbank, Yell, to John Walker, Maryfield, Bressay, October 1867.

During the late 1850s Thomas Penney, who tenanted Keldabister farm in Bressay, found himself sliding into debt and less able, as he aged, to cope with farming. He decided to give up the lease, possibly hoping that he could hand it on to his son; but in the event the farm was taken by an Aberdonian, John Walker. Walker had been recommended by the Rev Hamilton, minister of Bressay, which says much for the former's plausibility (he had no farming experience) and rather less for Mr Hamilton's ability to judge character (although as events would show he would be neither the first nor the last to be misled).

Walker arrived in Shetland in the spring of 1860. He immediately began the building of a large farmhouse in Bressay, a work undertaken without the permission of the estate, which had to pay for it. In the meantime he, with his family, resided in Lerwick, where he promptly refused to pay the Poor Law levy, and, upon being taken to court, successfully intimidated the organs of justice, unused as they apparently

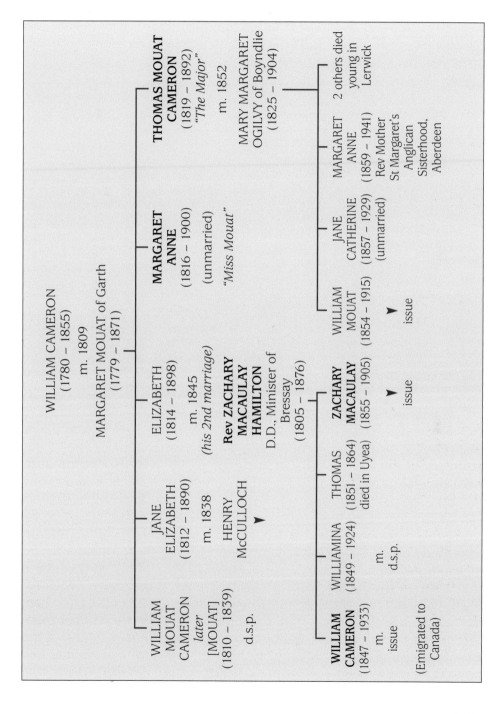

WILLIAM CAMERON
(1780 – 1855)
m. 1809
MARGARET MOUAT of Garth
(1779 – 1871)

THOMAS MOUAT CAMERON
(1819 – 1892)
"The Major"

m. 1852

MARY MARGARET
OGILVY of Boyndlie
(1825 – 1904)

MARGARET ANNE
(1859 – 1941)
Rev Mother
St Margaret's
Anglican
Sisterhood,
Aberdeen

JANE CATHERINE
(1857 – 1929)
(unmarried)

WILLIAM MOUAT
(1854 – 1915)

issue

2 others died
young in
Lerwick

MARGARET ANNE
(1816 – 1900)
(unmarried)
"Miss Mouat"

ELIZABETH
(1814 – 1898)
m. 1845
(his 2nd marriage)
Rev ZACHARY MACAULAY HAMILTON
D.D., Minister of
Bressay
(1805 – 1876)

ZACHARY MACAULAY
(1855 – 1905)

issue

THOMAS
(1851 – 1864)
died in Uyea

JANE ELIZABETH
(1812 – 1890)
m. 1838
HENRY
McCULLOCH

d.s.p.

WILLIAMINA
(1849 – 1924)
m.
d.s.p.

WILLIAM
MOUAT
CAMERON
later
[MOUAT]
(1810 – 1839)
d.s.p.

WILLIAM CAMERON
(1847 – 1933)
m.
issue

(Emigrated to
Canada)

were to such a self-confident and forceful defendant. Once installed in his new house, he abandoned the name Keldabister, naming house and farm Maryfield, evidently after his wife.

The farm steading at Maryfield farm showing Maryfield House in the background.

Walker immediately became active in local affairs. He was clerk to the Bressay District Road Committee, agent for the Scottish Fire Insurance Committee (whom he overcharged commission) and secretary of the short-lived Shetland Agricultural Society. On the farm itself he enthusiastically embraced innovation, with fields improved by the first tile drains installed in Shetland (still working well 150 years later).

If this flurry of productive activity was designed to recommend him to his landlord, it succeeded. Major Cameron was in the market for an able administrator to undertake the administration of his estates and to put them on a business footing. Walker's energy may have appealed. Major Cameron was physically worn out after the strain of the past years in India. But unfortunately for the people whose lives were about to be touched by these two men, neither possessed any understanding of the island communities in which they held authority nor, it seems, any beyond a simplistic view of estate management in Shetland.

When some years later the North Yell schoolteacher and surveyor John Houston gave evidence to the Truck Commission, he stated that with rising prices in the 1860s "a tenant could pay his rent at once with an animal, when he could not do that before".[1] Fishing tenures had largely disappeared, certainly on the larger estates where a money economy was now the norm. On Major Cameron's Garth and Annsbrae lands the system in the north had simply collapsed during his father's time (a fact later confirmed by Zachary Macaulay Hamilton[2]); while Bressay, adjacent to the economic mecca of Lerwick, had paid money rents from the late 1830s.

More generally, however, conditions in Shetland, where seasonal work was in many places coupled with an inevitably small volume of trade, contributed to the replacement of one credit arrangement by another – the so-called truck system, whereby a merchant bought the fish and provided stores and equipment on his own monopoly terms.[3]

Houston, who was well acquainted with the relationship between proprietor and fishcurer, and with the fishermen too, believed that poverty was the root cause of the continuing use of truck, but poverty's fellow was the subdivision of holdings:

> The islands being over-populated and the farms so insignificantly small, it follows as a result that the inhabitants have to depend on external aid, and throw themselves, although reluctantly it may be, into the arms of a system which, however honestly conducted, has a tendency to hamper their movements, to bereave them of independence, and to plunge parents and their children into debt...

He considered that cash payment to fishermen at the end of the summer season would virtually eliminate the situation where the fishermen were:

> ... dependent on their curer's store for months after the fishing closed ... the fisherman who has neither money nor credit must go to his curer's store, as he has no other alternative, but were he put in possession of his earnings at the close of the fishing, truck for a time would disappear from his individual horizon.[4]

Houston's analysis correlates significantly with the findings of Balfour of Trenaby a century earlier.[5]

By 1860 a large rural population was crammed onto every available parcel of land, much of it highly marginal, and worked in the age-old fashion. Runrig lands were often tiny – in Upper Scatsta about twenty-one acres were divided into thirty-six parts with a mill the "common property of the township" (May 1866). The people, in short, were trying to support themselves from manifestly inadequate resources. By now, however, large estates were trying to abolish the subdivision of farms, or, rather, to re-establish viable, larger, units. This aim, reasonable as it may have been, left unresolved the fate of the surplus population.

1867 proved a watershed year in the annals of Major Cameron's lands in Yell, Delting and Unst. John Walker was empowered to run and to rationalise them. He came straight up against the tenets of immemorial habit, custom and blood – it may be doubted whether he even recognised them. And the people found themselves challenged, their homes in danger. They were not, however, unwarned. The previous year Walker had issued new regulations for the lease and running of their farms, accompanied by a letter from Major Cameron giving Walker authority "in all matters concerning your farm".

Walker's regulations were based on the standard terms of agricultural leases (no off-farm sale of straw, hay, turnips or dung, compensation at the end of the lease, etc.), familiar to any farmer working improved land under lease, but new to unimproved lands, and in any case only workable on economically viable holdings. The stringency of the terms about improvement, crop rotation and summer fallow hardly allowed for the small size and marginality of many units (perhaps not entirely coincidentally). Some struck directly against custom, significantly the loss of scattald rights except for boats' noosts.

One hundred years previously William Balfour had shown how the farmers of Shetland depended upon their scattald for grazing for animals and peats for firing.[6] This situation still obtained, and was entirely understood. When in 1815 the division of commonties had been identified by the Shetland Society as essential for agricultural improvement, itself essential to feed a growing population, scattald rights were taken for granted, and division would not – and did not, in fact – alter this.

The necessity for divided commonties became clear as live animal exports from Shetland gradually assumed economic importance, and local sales, where crofters' beasts were readily bought by the bigger farms, provided a cash boost to family income. The scattald was an essential component of this arrangement, since there was insufficient grazing without it. It needed regulation, however, because before division there was no mechanism for checking the number of animals which could be grazed by any individual, a situation productive of overstocking, overgrazing, a constant problem of straying animals and hence the spread of disease, and no possibility of selective breeding.

Walker's attempt to forbid the use of the scattald was a different matter: it threatened the entire basis of a way of life. Cultivation of inbye land, which was unfenced, could not take place if animals were not out at the hill, and in any case, the small size of many smallholdings meant that they could not provide enough grazing for stock. The people needed their scattald; Walker's aim was to have the land available for sheep runs.

Walker in fact seems to have made a fallacious comparison with Orkney. Although the sheep farms he created remained viable units, benefiting as they did from a growing trade in sheep exports and increased prices following the introduction of sale by auction in 1872, it may be that he miscalculated the profitability of sheep farms where Blackface and Cheviot breeds were introduced (mostly in Delting); nor did he know enough about agriculture to understand that only the native Shetland breed was hardy enough to survive unfed on the overgrazed scattalds of the north. The marginal nature of much land, especially in Yell, remained a factor whether it was farmed or crofted, and profitability plummeted when the initial flush of fertility was exhausted.

It was the misfortune of the time that Walker's rules were never challenged by anyone competent to do so, and in particular, by Major Cameron, the only person with the authority to rein Walker in. But Major Cameron knew nothing of agriculture, and was determined to avoid involvement with his tenants to an extent which constitutes an abrogation of responsibility. Direct appeals were ignored by him, and letters passed straight on to Walker.

Walker, therefore, held unchecked authority on Garth and Annsbrae lands in Delting, Yell and Unst. The mindset there was itself depressed and conservative, worn down by years of hardship; never a promising recipe for withstanding an aggressive external challenge. There was an instinctive reversion to outdated methods, like the suggestion of John Spence's fledgling trading company in Unst that the tenants should be forced to fish for them, a suggestion rubbished by Walker: "they must bind their tenants to fish for them by other inducements than compulsion" (August 1866); and evident, too, in the response of the small farmers – the term "crofter" did not come into use until 1882 – who confronted Walker in August 1866 when he went to inspect the scattalds at Caldback Ness in Delting, but had nothing to suggest, when asked, but that things should not change: "... they did not like the idea of a lease nor the loss of the hill but said they would pay double their rent *to be allowed to remain as at present*." (My emphasis). One among them spoke the heart of the tragedy: "if we expected that they could pay as much as the land would (pay) if in sheep we were mistaken ..." (August 1866).

The result in human terms of outmoded ways, poverty and overpopulation was summed up, all unknowing, by 14-year-old Osla Barbara Irvine, of Kirkabister in North Yell. "I cannot write never having been to school,"[7] (August 1867). A generation growing up illiterate, without skills or opportunities, is a standing reproach to the effects of the status quo.

The house at Leiraness, Bressay, painted in 1883. Tuberculosis became a serious threat in overcrowded housing conditions. The Anderson family who lived here lost mother and four children from the disease. They eventually moved out of the house to get away from infection, and built a new house further up the voe, sometime between 1880 and 1901, but several more family members in the next generation also died of TB.

Into this uneasy state Walker cut like a knife. His style of dealing with people was heartily disliked. "... so very decided and dictatorial", grumbled Alexander Sandison, a view seconded elsewhere. The Edinburgh lawyer Henry Cheyne wrote to Major Cameron about the "loud complaints in regard to poundings made and threatened by Mr Walker ... of cattle belonging to Busta tenants, when the division of scattald had not yet been finally or legally determined".

Walker was well aware of the effect he had on people. "... of course I kick lustily and threaten much", he commented to Major Cameron in August 1868. Perhaps more harmful than threats was his devious way of behaving, which sowed a fatal seed of bad faith and distrust. He was a difficult man to tie down. "... we heard of you making rapid transit across this district," wrote one Yell resident in May 1867, a comment reiterated by many others. Invisible and threatening, he readily inspired fear.

Some tried to appeal over his head. Samuel Johnson, of Westafirth in Yell, wrote to Major Cameron in February 1867:

> Mr Walker called on me about my balance and I told him I had nothing to meet it with but my cattle, that an account of them was sent you some time ago. He asked me who had done it, I said Mr Houston. He said he would like to know who had the business to give such authority to Mr Houston, that it could not stand. I said I would lay my case before yourself. Mr Walker asked me if I would go to Graven to pay £5-10/- of rent and 15/- draining or fencing and also the poor rates. Although I am poor I need not be dishonest by promising what I can never perform. Mr Henderson has offered to give me shelter at Gloup and some land also. I must leave just now or another will get it; and as it appears that Mr Houston has no business to look after my cattle or the cattle of others I must trouble yourself to say to whom I am to give them. They are yours and you have been too kind to me that I should allow your subject to suffer, you may depend I will not. Mr Henderson may relieve one of them to take with me. I wish you to accept of my heartfelt thanks for the kindness and leniency so long shown to me, and may God bless you and yours.

Had he but known it, the letter went straight to Walker.

Direct appeals to Walker himself were frequent. William Gray of Infield, Delting, wrote:

> Having expected you at Infield this last two months I feel greatly disappointed as go I must by this boat but somehow by your appearance

> I have every confidence that you will do my mother every justice although at present she is sore afflicted and deprived of her earthly protector. It's my desire to do all I can for my mother and sisters but with an additional rent and without the island no-one can ever stop in Infield.

Gray was to be disabused. With William safely out of the way, Walker appeared at Infield in early March. He told Mrs Gray the rent would be £35 – "a very high rent," commented William, adding that "the leaving of Infield would be the means of throwing my poor mother into destitution" (16 March).

With the courage of desperation Mrs Gray hung on through the summer, "taking forcible possession of a portion of the land which belonged to her prior to the cutting of the division lines, other families followed her ...", and that September she negotiated a year's lease of Infield and the isle of Linga for a rent of £30. But it did not last. By November 1867 Infield was empty.

That same spring William Pole at Greenbank also wrote Walker, but softly, softly, since he had his eye on the grazing at Papil Ness:

> I heard from my sister at Garth lately. They appear to be very fraid [sic] and think they might not be able to keep up a sort of establishment for themselves for any time ... but are to... have it decided first time you are at Garth.

Pole wrote again on 6th March, his sister having been offered Millburn:

> ... they may not be able to keep together for any length of time... there is noone to succeed them. The place is very small and I understand could not produce crop sufficient to feed one cow during winter. Still I shall feel obliged if you could give them the place without a lease... I will look after the payment of the rent ...

Walker's intimidatory techniques wore everyone down. Even Alexander Sandison,[8] who with some others saw opportunity in the elimination of the small farms, found Walker exhausting to deal with. He seems to have misjudged Walker, making a series of demands about the new farm created (23rd September 1866) from the holdings of Thomas Gray, George Henderson and Bruce Fordyce[9] in Uyeasound, Unst. He asked for a discount on the first year's rent since "some of the ground is sore wasted". In addition: "I should like the dyke commenced as soon as possible, and think a 4 foot dyke is quite sufficient ... I have no fear you will arrange about putting up a small steading ..."

By January 1867, however, he commented to Walker "whether designedly or otherwise you so dampen me about taking on the place that you almost drive energy out of a fellow".

Others too took time to realise what ball game they were in. George Henderson at Burravoe, with whom Walker dealt in September 1866 regarding the division of the Gloup scattald, was quite ready to do so. "I have told my tenants that their right of pasturage bewest that burn firth ceases at Martinmas, in fact there was only occasionally quays[10] and horses of theirs that went there in summer and sweetly have they paid for it as 2 or 3 of the former fell over the wester lee last year ..." adding, candidly, "... your North Yell foxes are all a fickle set I well know ..."

But the scale and effects of the new rents and regulations began to cause alarm. By December 1866 Henderson himself was standing surety for William Henry "being warned to leave the farm he now holds in Lumbasta [sic] at Martinmas first 1867 (much against his will)" for his £9 debt to Major Cameron.

At Cullivoe Peter Sandison was closely in touch with events, and prepared to intercede. He wrote Walker on behalf of "your tenant in Kirkabister Laurence Williamson asking if you will let him the farm of Stonsetter as he understands he has to leave Kirkabister. He would take it at once ..." But a month later Williamson was still in search of a farm, this time at Stenster. "He came to Gloup to meet you," wrote Pennie, Walker's ground officer[11], "but you was off ... I know he is able to pay the rents ... he would like to know before you can be in Yell."[12]

Pennie too passed on many an anxious message, including Laurence Williamson asking to thrash part of his crop at Kirkabister – "the harvest will be very late" – and one of many, Alexander Williamson asking to remain at Vollister since "he has no place yet". Williamson was one of several "anxious to know if you would allow them a few days after the term to remove any crops that can't be got off in time, their cattle will be off but this late season they may not be able to clear all in time ..." (Pennie, 26 Sept), though luckier than some in that he was allowed to remain in Vollister and the house through the winter.

By this time it was understood that acting without permission brought retribution, so in September John Robertson put pen to paper to say "when you were at Swinister we were going to ask liberty to take a little earth from Foraness to put in our midding [sic] but you went away sooner than we expected ... please say if we can take any or not, we shall be sure not to take any with grass on it."

Peter Sandison wrote again on 20th September about David Williamson, the tenant at Brake of Houlland, who "wishes to stop as long as you will allow him, he was in Lerwick when you were here ... is a good tenant."

It was probably Sandison, who obviously liked David Williamson, who helped him to compose and write his letter to Walker:

> I am in receipt of your letter of 20th inst requesting me to call upon you on Friday 27th to arrange regarding my farm for next year.
>
> When you were lately at Cullivoe I was from home and was not aware that you wished the Tenants (who were to stay and who had cut their peats and made other necessary preparations for the winter) to call upon you. Had any intimation from you to that effect reached me it would have been punctually attended to by me. You will be pleased to favour me and treat me similarly as your other remaining tenants. I am physically unable to go to Lerwick by land and as the weather is so very coarse the 'Alice' is not expected here in time to reach Lerwick on Friday. I am not sensible of having given any offence either by word or deed and it is my wish to remain a tenant of Major Cameron as long as I can pay my rent and I trust you will not remove me or treat me differently from the other remaining tenants.

This produced an offer of a lease for another year.

Sandison's covering letter (2nd October) gives an indication of the fear which John Walker now inspired.

> He [David Williamson] came here this morning before I got up and I told him I should under the circumstances take his signature and send [it] on to you ... I hope you will allow the poor fellow to sit ... but I gave David distinctly to understand that you might refuse his signature as it was not signed on the day you mentioned.

The anger, powerlessness and pathos of the people, who found Major Cameron blind and deaf to any appeal, manifested itself in empty threats, sustained episodes of vandalism, and a dumb refusal to tell or do anything to assist Walker or his agents. But beyond that they were bereft of ideas. No leaders emerged to channel protest into more productive channels. That Walker rapidly inspired distrust amongst others is very clear. When he had to deal with Edinburgh solicitors one and all smelt a rat. Henry Cheyne, involved with scattald divisions, warned Walker:"I must entreat that you do not for a moment in any matters of this kind assume with me silence to be consent."

Sheriff Robert Bell, who had acquired the Lunna estates by marriage, wrote from Falkirk to decline further joint fencing deals with Walker. "I can scarcely accede to your proposal of ordering the Lunna tenants to land the [fencing] materials, for they have always been paid for any such labour..."

Later that year Bell wrote Walker again about his habit of illegally poinding poor folk's cattle. H. G. Dickson, acting for the Earl of Zetland, wrote from his office in Dundas Street, Edinburgh, pointing out to Major Cameron that in a projected scattald division he (for which undoubtedly read Walker) had failed to act properly: "communications as yet having been confined to a description of fence which you have no legal right to call upon Lord Zetland to concur with you in erecting".

A few days later, just round the corner in Heriot Row, old John Phin, who had handled the legal affairs for Garth and Annsbrae for more than thirty years, and was now kept very distant by Walker from estate business (but could not be got rid of since Miss Mouat at Gardie House continued to use him), wrote in similarly restrained legalese to express surprise "to hear of the recent setting of march stones in connection with the disputed boundary".

Phin continued:

> ... You will no doubt take care to preserve evidence of the time within which the stones must have been set, and the date at which you caused their removal ... the circumstance of your interfering with march stones at all, might be referred to as a probable way in which old march stones had disappeared, if it should be for the interest of anyone to say so. (1st August 1867).

Major Cameron might have considered all of this, as he read the fiery response of the ageing J. T. Irvine from Bath (March 1867) to Walker's letter about scattald boundaries.

> I have received sundry papers from you and an order from you to sign the same. I am utterly unaware of any possible right you have to order me in any manner. I return you the papers. Request you to consider it an end of our correspondence.

Walker, faced with an opponent he could not threaten, had complained to his boss. With extraordinary folly Major Cameron wrote to Irvine himself, eliciting another furious response (3rd April):

> I respectfully beg to deny that you have any right to term my letter to J Walker as 'discourteous' to yourself, your name never having been mentioned in it nor yourself referred to in the slightest degree ... I will not exterminate my countrymen, I have sins enough to answer for before Almighty God, and I appeal to his judgement, but that I am free of any hand airt or part in the matter, when he shall require it. You have my reply and you will see it is final.

In Unst, too, the Walker effect was plainly felt. Alexander Sandison realised what rationalisation entailed (February 1867): "... there is a fearful cry against us all here just now. The reports that are flying about would frighten any but a strong mind. It is quite as bad now in Unst against us as ever it was against you in other places." No one knew when or where the axe would fall.

"I learnt *in an indirect way*," (my emphasis) wrote Erasmus Bruce, who had lived on his Unst holding for 24 years, "that another tenant has taken the whole place next year." He reminded Walker of Miss Mouat's promise "that if ever I had to leave Houlland she should give me a house" (May 1867).

Meanwhile the letters came in, pleading for time as time ran out. William Spence wrote from Woodwick that March:

> I have got no place to go to as yet, I now ask you if it could be in your power to grant me the liberty of stopping in this house through the winter after Martinmas 1867 or if it should be but part of the winter for the purpose of consuming my crop and which would give me time to consider or look about me till I see how I might be suited.

From Bressay the Rev Hamilton, who had perhaps come to regret his initial recommendation, wrote to intercede for Spence: "I feel sure he will not presume on such allowance."

But Robert Bruce at Uyasound promised in vain that "on or after Martinmas first I shall carry on no business on the premises either in buying or selling unless with your permission, only as I have no other means of support and unable from bodily weakness for any other work I will trust to you for some other way of doing." That September Bruce received a summons of warning. "I do not know what effect it is having on him," wrote Alexander Sandison, "but I hear they are all going down by the packet."

Others too decided enough was enough, like Donald Anderson, who left Scatsta because of the high rent, and also "being obliged to bring home and store my peats at once which comes to be a very serious inconvenience..."

Onlookers watched with disquiet, like John Inkster from North Roe, who wrote to Walker that November:

> ... your intention of collecting rent to Andrew Moncrieff etc has been handed me. They having generally fished for me very naturally look to me to help them in their difficulties. They are honest men although not in very good circumstances. I shall do for them what I can and I think you can calculate on me paying their current rents in a week or two hence, as soon as I have done settling with fishermen. This will be a sad year ... both on tenants and proprietors. Grain getting up rapidly and low prices for produce. I regret to notice Major Cameron's intention of raising rents here as no other of the proprietors have done so and if the major's property is higher valued than other it is naturally to be supposed that the tenantry will try to better themselves by removing to other farms and it is really a pity to lose a good tenant for the sake of a few shillings. This however is a matter that does not concern me and my opinion is uncalled for...

Major Cameron continued to display a rigidity of mind perhaps as antipathetic in his own day as it appears now. After an incident of vandalism, when tar barrels were overturned on the beach by a couple of youths, Major Cameron, perhaps doubting the ferocity of the legal response, was ready to victimise the parents. He commented that whatever the Fiscal does "their father can be got at and punished by being turned off".

And it is instructive to read his comment on the valedictory appeal by Laurence Manson at Westafirth (October 1867):

> Your honour was so good as to say that while I could pay my rent I should not be put away and your honour can see by the book that I have always paid my rent and I have been a long time on your property and my forefathers before my day. And I would not have liked to have changed my landlord as long as I lived.
>
> I have a written agreement with Mr Walker for one of your farms in Cullivoe. But as Mr Walker gave me leave to labour in Westafirth I did so, and I expected to get the farm in Cullivoe whenever I had to leave Westafirth, but the farm in Cullivoe was given to another, and I have now no place to go to...

The letter ends with a request to graze his cattle at Westafirth. At the foot of the letter Major Cameron wrote only: "This request as to grazing having been granted, asking me seems needless."

The net result of a year's anguish is William Pennie's letter of 21st December 1867: "I was at Kirkabister last night with the tups and got the sheep bathed less 28 owing to the bad weather and not getting the bath made up in time, I could not get them finished though I wrought with a lamp till past 8 o'clock on Saturday night ... ," an eerie feeling for Pennie working in the black dark with the silent houses empty around him.

Events in the north must have been followed with foreboding in Bressay. Walker had had no locus there although technically factor on Mrs Cameron Mouat's Garth lands. Her presence presented an absolute bar to the abuse of power. It is hardly surprising, therefore, that her death in July 1871, coupled with an announcement of new leases to be issued for the small farms, provoked an outbreak of collective hysteria in the island, strong enough that Major Cameron could not overlook it. His response was rapid and unambiguous. He sold the island to his sister Anne.

The question which comes to mind is the relationship between Major Cameron and his powerful employee. In spite of accumulating evidence of financial impropriety by Walker in virtually every operation with which he was involved – John Houston had challenged him as early as February 1869 ("Will you admit to making a false return? Or will you be prepared to prove that sheepfarming cannot afford the same rents as those paid by the former tenants?") – Major Cameron himself did not finally part company with him until 1875, a refusal to act which appears downright perverse.

Yet Major Cameron was not stupid. In fact he subsequently had a career in public life, gifting the site for St Magnus Episcopal Church in Lerwick, and becoming Convenor of Zetland County Council. But it is frequently to be observed, that those who enjoy such high-profile positions may, when faced with situations requiring moral courage, reveal themselves to be lamentably deficient. It was certainly so with Major Cameron.

When in 1872 Anne Cameron Mouat bought Bressay from her brother, John Walker was of course still tenant of Maryfield farm. Did Miss Mouat indicate to him that his continued presence was not welcome? Since she wrote few letters and estate documents have not survived, the details of what happened remain obscure. However, financial compensation was payable to Walker on relinquishing the farm (it contributed to the fortune of £20,000 which Walker is said to have accumulated during his years in Shetland[13]).

Miss Mouat herself certainly considered that she had got rid of Walker. If she paid over the odds it is doubly significant in view of her well documented stinginess in matters financial. Whatever happened, the Walker family moved back to Aberdeen, and although Walker continued to hold office in Shetland for several years to come, as factor, member of school boards etc., his power base had been eliminated.

As for Walker himself, his record is well attested, but he may have had more charm than appears from the documents. "I met him once," wrote the Shetland antiquarian E. S. Reid Tait:

> A daughter of his was married to the Rev Charles Stobie the minister of Whalsay and we were very friendly with the Stobies and used to exchange visits. In 1904, I think it was, I was making one of these visits ... and old John was there visiting his daughter. Now my father had, among countless others, been very friendly with him ...when he learnt

who I was he took a kindly interest in me. Of course knowing as I did all about him I was not very flattered but I must confess he had a wonderful personality." [14]

In a John Walker free Bressay, Miss Mouat, now aged 55, became independent for the first time in her life and able to make decisions without a guiding masculine hand to control her, one of very few Victorian women to find herself in that position.

She was not however inexperienced in estate affairs, having often acted for her mother since her father's death in 1855. Since then there had been some re-allocation or division of holdings and rents had been adjusted several times, both upwards and downwards, but always by small amounts; leases were not the norm, the farms of Keldabister, Noss and Setter being the exceptions. There was no question of eviction. Mrs Cameron Mouat would have been utterly opposed to any such thing.

Her death, and the brief but tumultuous intervention of John Walker, coincided with the final closure of the slate and flagstone quarries at Aith, which had, in previous years, employed all the men in the adjacent toun. This was the final blow to the economically active inhabitants of Aith, where the process of amalgamation of holdings had been slowly continuing since 1867, when the adjacent farm of Setter had been taken over by Simon Anderson. Anderson continued to acquire grazing land as the economic migration from the tounships continued. He retired to Orkney in about 1899 having amassed some 400 acres in all.

By 1874 the township of Aith, with the quarries shut, lost the eight families who had lived there. In a pattern which seems to have been replicated elsewhere in the island, the economically active went where there was work. Most of them can be traced to other holdings in Bressay, but some went to Lerwick. [15] The elderly were not displaced. They stayed on: Jean Gifford, a pauper, aged 70, who died in September 1872 and Barbara Yorston aged 90, in April 1876. [16]

Similarly at Cullisbrough and Noss Sound the touns emptied. Left to the old, when they died the hearths became cold for the last time. At Noss Sound, although the three holdings were all entered as vacant on the Valuation Roll of 1875/76, old James Linklater lived there till his death in March 1878, when his widow went to live with her married daughter at Uphouse. The land became pasture.

The new big farms needed workers. At Hoversta, small holdings were amalgamated to make the farm, but some families stayed in their homes and were employed on the farm; others moved to new crofts.[17] Meanwhile the pattern of consolidation acquired a momentum of its own; the units of Uphouse and Midgarth, previously held by the Rev Hamilton, were taken over by John Walker in 1873/74 and subsequently by his successor at Maryfield, the Marquis of Londonderry.

The Marquis of Londonderry's plaque.

John Walker had necessarily remained tenant of Maryfield till his lease expired, but by 1874 the farm was occupied by the Marquis of Londonderry, or rather his manager, J. J. R. Meiklejohn. Meiklejohn was keen to acquire as much grazing land as possible for the Shetland ponies being reared for Londonderry's coal mines in the north of England. There were 400 breeding mares on the island of Noss, where a careful breeding programme laid the foundation of the modern Shetland pony stud.[18]

Meiklejohn employed several local men, among them Andrew White, who began as a ploughman at Maryfield, and was later employed to look after the ponies on the east side grazings at Noss Sound and

Ponies at the Voehead, Bressay, and being landed in Lerwick. © *Shetland Museum*

Culliesbrough; it is told that he came from his home at Noss Sound over the hill to Culliesbrough to milk a mare for a child as a remedy for the whooping cough (two babies are recorded as dying in late 1894-early 1895 from whooping cough).[19]

The changes which occurred in Bressay in the 1870s continued into the closing decades of the 19th century. It is clear, however, that they differed from the upheavals instituted by Walker on Garth and Annsbrae lands in the north.

In Bressay the people can be traced in all except a few cases; none were left homeless and once Bressay came into the hands of Miss Mouat a programme of house building began, in terms substantially the same as her informal missive of lease issued to Alexander Tait and Laurence Laurenceson in 1873:

> I now according to my promise grant to you both a lease of the 4 ½ acres of ground, outside the Hill Dykes of Ham, on which I gave you permission to build your present houses on the following conditions, viz – that you enclose the ground with a good and sufficient stone dyke, 'sheep hadden', that you make and keep everything neat and nice looking during your lease ... that you neither sublet any part of your lease, nor permit a shop in it, nor anything subversive of good order, and the most strict propriety. For this you are to pay 10/- each for one fire, and 1/- per acre. Peats to be cut, cured etc according to the rules to be observed on the Property. Wishing you both well, and much comfort to you both in your new houses.

By 1881 Miss Mouat had granted leases on 18 outsets on pieces of common taken out of the hill; these were "under lease of 19 years and less than 57 years", paying an average rent of 12/-, the houses' yearly rent or value varying from £1 to £4 for those with slated roofs.

The reason for this difference lies fundamentally in Bressay's position adjacent to Lerwick. There were money jobs there, and a harbour which was first port of call for the whalers coming in to pick up crew on their way north. The tale of Willie Laurenson, who went out from his home at The Burns to fetch water from the well, saw the incoming vessel with the flag flying which meant crew wanted, and was next seen six months later, may be apocryphal, but is illustrative.

Census returns show how, although the backbone of the island continued to be small holdings, many of them were home to grown-up family who worked outwith the croft, usually as seamen and fishermen, although Bressay men, noted for their skill as stone masons, found employment in booming Lerwick building houses, schools, and the new Town Hall, which opened in 1883.

As the employment profile of Bressay diversified, people were no longer tied to the tyranny of the smallholding. By 1880/81 houses are entered on the valuation roll without land, reflecting the move away from the days of subsistence "farming", and also evident from the description of people with money jobs, from the large number of seamen to such diverse things as gardeners, schoolteachers, and skilled tradesmen, and the herring boom saw the number of full-time fishermen in Bressay rise from seven to thirty-eight.

Other efforts were made to promote employment. The 1880s saw the beginnings of the proliferation of fishing stations along the shore of Bressay Sound, and the building of a "fishing village" at Ham, for which Miss Mouat provided the infrastructure – a pier, a road and four houses, built to a high standard by Orkney masons. The houses were mostly filled by fishing families from Inverallochy, who provided their own boats and gear and fished on their own behalf. They were now using bigger decked boats but the economics of fishing remained precarious and in the longer term commercial fishing from Bressay ceased.

Miss Mouat lived at Gardie House. She kept little correspondence and her reaction to changing times is unknown; she donated a stained glass window and one of the bells for the new Town Hall in Lerwick. She was a keen gardener, and under her instructions trees and herbaceous plantings were laid out in the gardens round the house, many of which have survived.

Tended by her niece May McCulloch, she lived on into a difficult and demanding old age, refusing to spend any money, neglecting the house, perhaps critical of her younger brother Major Cameron.

She is remembered locally as something of a tartar.[20] But to the end of her life she herself believed that she had followed the example set to her by her parents, in trying to act for the good of the people who lived on her property.

In a letter of March 1896 she wrote:

> ... from the very first of my having anything to do with Bressay, from the saving the people's being sent adrift by John Walker, to every improvement that followed, either to the people body and mind, or to the homes I had preserved to them, and up to the present time, in every way in my power, I have gladly laid out both time and means on the improvement of Bressay ...

M. A. Cameron's painting of a Dutch broom aground in Lerwick, with Twageos House on right and Bressay in the background, 1891.

Dutch Broom aground. AC. 25.6.91.

By the time of Miss Mouat's death, however, the old system had ended with the passing of the 1886 Crofters Act.

Shetland's small farmers were now designated crofters, with absolute security of tenure. The setting of a fair rent by the government took power definitively out of the hands of the landlord. In Shetland fair rents were not assessed until 1892, when the Napier Commission arrived at last to take evidence. In the intervening years most tenants simply stopped paying rent at all.

Zachary Macaulay Hamilton, factor to the Garth Estate, giving evidence to the Commission at Baltasound, stated that at Martinmas 1885, total arrears in Unst amounted to £139-1-8, of which about half were "really bad debts which should have been written off many years before"; in 1888, two years after the passing of the Act, arrears in Unst came to £1156-17-2. "Some of the crofters had the honesty to tell me," he said, "they could pay their rent in full but they would not do so until they saw what the Commission would do." What the Commission did do was to reduce practically all estate rents, and to wipe all arrears. Rents and holdings, thus fossilised, remained unchanged for more than half a century.

The result of this was entirely foreseeable. Estate income plummeted. Crofting rents, which of course remained static as the pound devalued, formed an ever smaller proportion of the money needed to run the estate, not so much of a problem on big Highland estates with absentee landlords and extensive sporting rights, but nearly impossible for Garth. The estate was still legally liable for repairs to tenants' houses and property. As is often the case with overtly punitive legislation, the result was to penalise the people who were supposed to benefit. Estate investment simply stopped. It was now impossible to finance the building of good quality houses like the ones Miss Mouat had built in Bressay. Since no-one else was building houses, the result was to leave far too many people for far too long in poor quality accommodation.

In 1886, however, crofters rightly celebrated a legal status ensuring their security from arbitrary eviction, and the new lower rents were now set in stone. But some at least must have realised that other problems remained. The pattern of small holdings was now fossilised, but it did nothing to stem the move off the land. The Shetland population continued to fall.

NOTES:

1   Zachary Macaulay Hamilton, minister of Bressay, whose son Zachary later became factor to Garth and Annsbrae.
2   Zachary Macaulay Hamilton, evidence to the Crofters Commission, Unst, 1892.
3   James R. Coull, *Shetland, the land, sea, and human environments* (Shetland's Northern Links, Language and History, ed Doreen J Waugh).
4   John Houston, Evidence to the Truck Commission, 1872.
5   See Chapter 3.
6   See Chapter 3. Balfour had also pointed out that where scattalds were overused, they were of no benefit to anyone.
7   Wendy Gear *John Walker's Shetland.* p 64.
8   Alexander Sandison of Lund (1827-1900), moved to Unst in 1858 and founded the firm of Sandison Brothers in fish curing and general merchandise; his brother Peter was a merchant at Cullivoe, Yell.
9   Thomas Gray, whose house at Roonan became the ploughman's house, moved to Midayre, where he had a small holding of 2 ½ acres round the site of the present Uyeasound Hall. George Henderson did not move out of his house at West Musselburgh, where the 1881 census recorded him as "retired". Bruce Fordyce also stayed in his house and is entered as a cooper in the 1871 census.
10 Quay, quoy - heifer

NOTES:

11   William Pennie (1832-1891) son of Thomas, who had come to Shetland from Aberdeenshire and was tenant of Keldabister farm in Bressay; William worked for a time as grieve to John Walker in Bressay; later he was promoted to the farm at Windhouse in Yell and acted as general factotum for Walker, before leaving his employment to become shepherd on Uya Isle, Unst.

12   Laurence Williamson's wife "prevented him from assisting" etc – one of the resistances to John Walker in Yell. But they still needed a farm.

13   E.S.Reid Tait to N.O.M. Cameron, 20th November 1954.

14   Ibid.

15   The 1851 census shows that all the male tenants in Aith worked at the quarries. Ten years later the younger men had gone to sea and others had died. As the active young left, they were not replaced; Setter farm took over the land and the houses were lived in by the single – and poor – elderly.

16   The story that the last inhabitants of Aith, two widows, went to the peat hill and on their return found their roof ablaze and so were forced to move does not appear to correlate with the census records and valuation rolls.

17   Several families lived on the land which became Hoversta farm. Several stayed, probably continuing to work the land now as farm servants. All the others moved to holdings nearby; several got pieces of common and built new houses, like Willie Tait and his son-in-law who together built the houses now called Seaview. It seems quite often to have happened that even if the land itself was taken into the farm, the folk in their houses stayed where they were (eg Barbara Hunter and her daughter, the Yorston families, the Smiths at Cowgate, and the Giffords at Gunhall). Many of the men were now entered on the census returns as seamen.

18   The pony pund built in Noss was one of four in Shetland, all on Garth Estate land; the others are at Garth and Dalesvoe in Delting, and Kirkabister in Yell.

19   The late Willie Manson, ploughman at Maryfield Farm, pers com.

20   The late Peter Manson of Mizpah, Bressay, pers com.

CHAPTER SEVEN

THE BISHOP

> *I have just come in from the hill (5.30am) and am*
> *wearing oilskins as we cannot leave the sheep any time.*
> *I have been 34 years at lambings but this one beats*
> *anything I ever saw – not a blade of grass come yet.*
>
> Zachary Macaulay Hamilton, Unst, to the
> Rev. William Cameron, Isle of Wight, 29th April, 1905.

When Major Thomas Cameron died in December 1892 his son William was an Anglican curate in Guildford, Surrey. This short-lived appointment – he was there only for three years – was the beginning of an English period in a life lived mostly abroad. Born in India, William's early experiences included the turmoil of the Great Mutiny of 1857. He was seven when his family came home to Shetland and a teenager when he left again, to continue his education begun at the Anderson Institute, Lerwick, at Loretto in Edinburgh and then Uppingham School in Buckinghamshire.

There he flourished, becoming Captain of School and winning a scholarship to Corpus Christi College, Oxford. But his health had never been robust – it was partly because of that that he had been sent away from Shetland for his schooling and, in accordance with contemporary medical wisdom, he was sent by his doctors to the south of France. Cannes bored him; but his doctor there suggested he visit North Africa, where he discovered an old school friend was English Chaplain in Algiers.

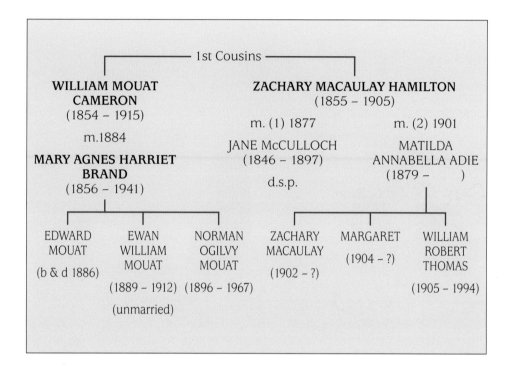

He was readily accepted into the small but lively expatriate community, and began the habit of solo journeys into unknown country which was to last a lifetime.

The hot weather suited him; his health improved; and he turned increasingly to the beliefs of the Anglican church for comfort and guidance as he pondered the question of his future. At Cherchel, ancient capital of Mauretania, where he viewed the tomb of Cleopatra Selene, daughter of the famous queen of Egypt, he commented on a Roman sarcophagus:

> ... the device on it [was] meant for the Good Shepherd, though not quite according to our ideas of good taste ... the wavy lines, associated in our minds with Renaissance and therefore heathen architecture, and therefore not likely to be found now on any tomb where good taste is exercised, are quite in place on a real Roman sarcophagus, so one need not be surprised, though one would not imitate the example, at finding the Good Shepherd represented in Roman dress.

Rev Cameron's house at Umtata, South Africa. St John's Boys School with Rev Cameron headmaster. July 1882.

142

By the summer of 1879 he was in South Africa, where he took Holy Orders, and became a curate at St John's Cathedral, Umtata. The English church in South Africa was committed at that time to active missionary work with a strong educational component, work in which they cooperated with the nonconformist missions. Efforts were being made to persuade the local tribes to allow the setting up of schools and training colleges.

One such meeting Rev Cameron described in a letter of October 1878:

> ... perhaps 500 of the Pondomisi appeared, some in clothes and some in blankets, with their woolly hair dressed in the most varied and often fantastical shapes. A favourite way seemed to be to let it grow long on the top of the head and cut it in the shape of a cone without its point. This looks rather like a chignon but I was told it was all real hair... several of the chief men of the tribe spoke, among them Umpelile, an old man, their great witchdoctor, the nearest thing to a priest that they have, who on the pretext of witchcraft causes the death of many rich but innocent men ... the Bishop had an interesting meeting with natives near Kokstadt, who asked for missionaries, and teaching. They do not want their children to grow up as they have done ... after the chiefs had spoken, another man got up to show that it was not the chiefs only, but the people that wanted teaching.

In spite of these initiatives, South Africa was the scene of endemic warfare. Cameron was aware of the dangers, and accepted them: "So long as I do not run into danger uncalled, I think I may trust with all confidence to God's protection, or at any rate, that if anything apparently harmful should happen to me, that a greater good is intended to result from it to us all," he wrote to his father, with the gentle but absolute faith which was now his.

In October 1880 sections of the Pondomisi tribe cut down a group of Europeans including the Resident Magistrate. Warned by a local minister who had managed to escape the massacre, a party of Christians both European and native, including Rev. Cameron, took refuge in the prison at Tsolo, which was stonebuilt. Local people surreptitiously passed food and water in through the loopholes at night and warned them against believing the blandishments of the leaders to get them to come out – "an impi of young men is waiting by the river to murder you all".

The besieged organised themselves to keep watch, share the food, keep the children happy; Rev. Cameron held twice daily services. After eight days of heat and tension a small relieving column pushed through the hills to lift the siege and take them through enemy lines to safety in Umtata.

The aftermath of this incident was that the chiefs involved, having duly served their prison sentences, now threw their weight behind the establishment of training colleges, to the extent of sending their sons for education there. Cameron had now decided about his future. "The climate here seems to suit me admirably", he wrote his father in February 1883; "Dr Johnson says "I doubt if you will be able to stand the Scotch climate long…" I know you will be very sorry to hear this… but it does seem in one way to make it clearer what one ought to do…" By this time he had been promoted within the church hierarchy, and had just moved from his post as headmaster of St John's School to that of Warden of the adjacent Training College.

Rev. Cameron would never have returned to Britain but for his marriage. In 1884, whilst home on leave, he met and married Mary Brand, the daughter of an Edinburgh solicitor (and, by a strange turn of fate, a great-granddaughter of that Charles Mitchell of Uresland who had been the Edinburgh agent of Magnus Henderson of Gardie). The Shetland Times of 15 November 1884 reported the wedding, which took place in St Mary's Cathedral, Edinburgh, in earnest detail. The bride's dress was of "cream duchesse satin trimmed with lace, orange-blossoms and Madina feather-flowers" – but the reporter became studiously vague when it came to the details of her bouquet, described, rather lamely, as "lovely white flowers". A fortnight later the Camerons sailed from Southampton for South Africa.

Mary was a lady of decided views and temperament, which extended to where she wanted to live; her views were reinforced by the hardships of the mission field faced with, or in the absence of, a husband who put duty first and family second. Africa killed the Camerons' first baby; by the time the second one arrived, in October 1889, Mary had prevailed upon her husband to return to England. For the Rev. Cameron the transition from his South African responsibilities to the blinkered complacency of Victorian Surrey was an abrupt one. His years of work, travel and responsibility counted for nothing. He became a curate again before securing his own parish at Ryde on the Isle of Wight. There the family settled; and there, in 1896, another son, Norman, was born to them.

It was during these quiescent years that Rev. Cameron found himself the owner of a Shetland property. His father had of course bequeathed him all his holdings; additionally, his Aunt Ann, Miss Mouat, now in her eighties, had a liferent of Gardie House in Bressay and various lands in Unst, and owned the island of Bressay, which however would revert to him at purchase price, if he wished to buy it. It is clear that the whole question of the Shetland connection was more of an anxiety than anything else.

"There is only one reason against letting Bressay go," wrote Mary Cameron to her husband's newly-appointed Edinburgh solicitor, Patrick Blair, in June 1893, "and that is that the house there is the only one we should ever care to live in ... I should never consent to living there all the year round, but *we* might manage it in the summer, if there were any strong reason for it. At the same time neither of us would care very much if we had to give up the idea of going up there at all."

These uncompromising views were perhaps not altogether shared by her husband. Rev. Cameron had family living in Shetland and, it may be hoped, had some good memories of the years of his boyhood spent running around the lanes and quays of Lerwick.

As far as his landed property went, he was far from indifferent to its proper management. Fortunately for all concerned, he was also good at picking the right people to act for him. Exasperated by the unbusinesslike habits of the Edinburgh solicitor John Torry, who had acted for both his aunt and his father, Rev. Cameron rapidly replaced him with Patrick Blair of the Edinburgh firm Blair and Cadell WS, thus ensuring competent professional advice. Since the Camerons themselves would not live in Shetland, he also needed a trustworthy factor to act for him. One was at hand. Almost Rev. Cameron's first act as proprietor, in 1893, was to appoint his first cousin and near contemporary, Zachary Macaulay Hamilton.

Zachary Macaulay Hamilton was the youngest of the numerous children of that Rev Zachary Macaulay Hamilton who had come to live in Bressay in 1833. After his father's death in 1876 young Zachary became his mother's mainstay, so that the option of emigration, which he found highly appealing, was not really realistic. Energetic, hard-working and sensible, he set out to make a living in Shetland, and soon obtained a lease of the farm at Symbister in Whalsay. He was able to supplement his

Belmont House in Unst shortly before Zachary Macaulay Hamilton built a new replacement front porch in 1899.

income by working as factor to Miss Mouat and also to his uncle, Major Cameron, succeeding John Walker in this role.

It is obvious from correspondence that Major Cameron had learnt nothing and understood still less from his experiences in Shetland. Zachary's approach in dealing with the ageing autocrat was tactful but firm, and unlike John Walker, he did understand his native islands. "I do not think it would do," wrote Zachary in May 1879, "to take A Smith as a yearly tenant for Scatsta [farm]", and proceeded to spell out the present state of affairs there:

> On all the old arable land which the tenants used to cultivate there is nothing whatever but rushes and thistles, so that the ewes have actually nothing but the hill, and of course they cannot do without a green bite of some sort. I have considered the matter well, and as far as I can see there are only two courses open to it, viz, to turn it in to wedders, or cultivate it and winter hoggs on it...

146

Zachary, with a practical interest in productive farming, chronicled the changing face of Shetland agriculture: "most of the small tenants are crossing their sheep with Cheviot and Blackface tups," he commented in June 1877. He found it difficult, however, to farm and factor simultaneously since the factor's job entailed so much time away from home, understanding well that "there is nothing can be really profitable unless one is on the spot oneself", but he did not allow the pressures to swamp his own sense of humour, nor his business acumen.

In June 1877 when settling his account with D Henderson of Halkirk in Caithness for wintering hoggs[1] he wrote: "... you will see by the above a/c that you are 1/9 in my debt which you can spend beside Mr Sutherland and drink my health with it. PS it was Mr N Gunn who said you had not done justice to my hoggs."

This cheerful finger-on-the-pulse approach inspired confidence; in spite of his views Zachary had the leases of both of Major Cameron's Delting farms, Garth and Swinnister, which he ran with farm managers, and he also made a spirited attempt to take on Noss and Maryfield in Bressay. This project fell through when his elder brother Willie refused to come in with him. (Willie, a much less sanguine character, had an unhappy career in Shetland and finally emigrated in 1888).

At the time of Major Cameron's death in 1892 Zachary's lease of Symbister was about to expire. Once again he considered going abroad. But that summer William Cameron came to Shetland, and the cousins walked over the Garth lands together – a process which, excluding various islands, took seven or eight days – took the measure of each other, and the bargain was sealed.

Rev. Cameron's attitude towards his Shetland estate was influenced by the fact that his interests and commitments lay elsewhere. He would not take the step of selling it – indeed, he bought back Bressay from his Aunt Ann in 1896 – instead, he would do his duty by it as best he could. He showed a real interest in his tenants; when in Shetland he always visited every house on his property; and one of the reasons for the successful partnership between Rev. Cameron and Zachary was that the latter was extremely good at keeping his cousin informed about the "people" side of events in Shetland.

Zachary's letters chronicle a community in the slow process of change. Public works began to impinge on private interest. In April 1897 the Rev Littlejohn Barr wrote from Bressay to describe the process of getting land for the new hall, a process not without difficulties:

> I have seen the man on whose croft we were proposing to build, but he refuses to give the sight [sic]... Mr Sutherland farmer in Hoversta has expressed his willingness to give a site in the field on the other side of the road exactly opposite the school... he will ask no compensation ...

In the south of Unst there was a move to build a reading room – a "People's Institute" – such as already existed at Baltasound. A public collection raised funds and Mr Sandison offered a site free, "but the majority of the promoters," wrote Zachary to Rev. Cameron, "would prefer a site on your ground about the middle of the beach... I have been requested to mention the matter to you. I said I felt quite sure you would give them a site, if they undertook to satisfy the claim of any tenant from whom the site was taken."

The 1886 Crofters Act and consequent drop in estate income meant it was difficult to fund house repairs. The details emerge from Zachary's correspondence. In March 1898 Laurence Smith, the ground officer in Bressay, wrote Zachary on behalf of Magnus Robertson about "getting his [house] repaired".

> He would like to know if it was to be done for he could be getting stones. He says that he will make all the help he can to lessen the expense. He wants a felt roof and the house a few feet longer. He says that he might get the masons before they began to the Church Hall..."

Zachary recommended that "you give him the material – wood, packssheet and tar, probable cost about £6 but insist on him doing the whole work himself. I am afraid if you do more than this you will have ever so many down on you for the same."

In the same letter:

> Widow Nelson [at] Brough was very anxious at settling time to have her house repaired and enlarged. I told her to get a competent man to say probable cost... she pays 10/- at present and I understand that she would willingly pay 30/- if the house was repaired and made 4ft longer. She is in good circumstances, being well left at least so report says.... The only (other) house requiring extensive repair in Bressay is John Smith's Brough. It has to get a new roof. I promised it two years ago but could never get men at the right season. It is very bad...

Zachary was a familiar figure on estate territory. In March 1898 he wrote:

> I have been all over the Westing today, you will notice in the rent roll I put in the margin John Johnston as the new tenant for the little house that Spence had for his mother at 7/-. I put John's rent at 20/- but he is increasing the size of the house and otherwise repairing it, which he is to leave without compensation, so I agreed the rent should be 14/- instead of 20/-. Margaret Cluness' house Underhoull is in a very bad state. She was out and I did not see her. She has plenty of means and if she had been a man I would have insisted on her repairing it, as she is bound to do under the Act. I'll see her soon, but I am afraid I won't make any impression on her. John Smith's Newgord roof is bad, and he wants to get a new wood and felt roof, I said I would advance him the material to be paid for in 3 years, but he would much prefer to get it and pay interest....

Continuing his tour of inspection, he wrote from Yell a fortnight later:

> ... old Widow Laurenson Caldback Delting is clear and her daughter was anxious to get away, so although I got no legal warning I allowed her to go. They paid £2. For this year I have got the Smiths (Widow Smith's sons) to take the land without the house at 35/-. I paid Widow Laurenson's daughter £4-6-3 compensation for inside plenishment in the house. It is good plenishing and I think will be well worth the money. I expect to get 50/- for house and land next year...

The following year he was in Bressay.

> Widow Anderson's house in Brough is in need of a new roof. All the other houses in Brough have been repaired at the proprietor's expense as the tenants did not apply to the Crofters Commission, and I think hers should be done too. Widow Gray, Uyeasound would also require a new roof. Her husband had he lived would have done it himself. She of course is unable to do it... she has a hard time of it, 7 bairns eldest 13.

October 1899:

> ...poor old Laurie Johnson of Sandale has had to give up his croft. He has no-one to help him but one girl. He is £7-7-9 in arrears, but he has acted honourably by refusing to sell anything off the croft without my sanction. I have let the croft to a very decent young man Gilbert Smith

and I went there with him last Monday and valued all Laurence's crop and a cow and calf... the total value of Laurence's stuff both out and in will be about £18... he has been a tenant for 51 years... he is going to a room at Uyeasound the rent of which is £1-10... I would suggest that... instead of giving him down any of his arrears you allow him to sit in the room rent free for 2 or 3 years...he has been very poorly all this summer...

Sometimes even Zachary met his match.

I have seen Margaret Clark and she says she will not pay interest on the repairs of her house. She says it is perfectly tight and comfortable. Her idea of tight and comfortable is different from other people's... she keeps calves, sheep and fowls in the house and is not happy unless she has them with her...

In late 1900 Zachary was in Bressay, and was approached by Jessie Gifford, "a most reputable woman", recently widowed, and "in a great state" since it appeared that her eldest son would be granted tenancy of her late husband's croft at Hoove. This decision would be made by the Crofters' Commission under the Act. The prospect not only dismayed his mother but her neighbours too, to the extent that a petition was raised locally against it.

Zachary decided to oppose the appointment, detailing his reasons in a letter to Rev Cameron – "1. If he gets the croft his mother and all the rest of the family must turn out. 2. His wife was convicted of theft a few weeks ago. 3. He is I believe an undischarged bankrupt". (The Crofters Act prohibited (Section 1 subsect (6)) bankrupts from tenanting crofts; Zachary asked "if that is so with the crofter it ought surely to be equally so with an aspirant to the croft?") 4. His coming to the Hoove would destroy the peace and quietness of the whole neighbourhood." Zachary's local solicitor was pessimistic about their chances of success, but Rev. Cameron, sympathetic as always to a human predicament, agreed that they should stand firm. In the event the Commission agreed a compromise, granting a joint tenancy which gave Jessie security for the rest of her life (she died in 1915).

Such were the problems which, regularly communicated by Zachary, kept Rev. Cameron in touch with life in Shetland. So did the weather reports that Zachary frequently included – "tonight we have about 2 inches wet snow on the ground, hardly any of the corn is in yet and the potatoes are rotting very fast" (10 October 1896), a comment which may well have caused Rev. Cameron to bless the medical condition which necessitated his living in a less rigorous climate.

"I notice you have included Basta [in the lease]", wrote Alex Sandison to Zachary in September 1899 about his holding in North Yell.

> I would rather you did not include it, for while we are willing to keep it from year to year at the present rent, with a year's notice to quit, we do not know how we can get on with it, being too small to stand the wages of a regular shepherd. We have had three years trial of it as a farm for ewes and lambs, have drained it etc, but the result is so poor and disheartening that we have resolved to give that up, and intend trying it with yield[2] or young sheep, only requiring a caretaker, who would not cost half a shepherd's wages...

And the quest for good tenants continued. There was little the estate could do about crofting tenants, but the farms were a different matter.

Zachary had cause to be pleased, in June 1899, when he agreed terms with Anderson Manson to take the tenancy of Maryfield farm in Bressay. "His family are unwilling to leave Shetland, and in his agreement he stipulates for a break at 5 years and says if he finds he can't make it pay he can give it up then."

Zachary was quite ready to agree Manson's insistence on exclusive use of the pier below the farmhouse at Maryfield, unless the weather prevented the crofters using the other pier at Mel. "Whether the place pays him or not," he wrote his cousin William with satisfaction, "he will pay what he promises and he will keep the place tidy and nice, so it will be a credit both to you and himself."

The task of running the estate was complicated for Zachary and his cousin by their Aunt Ann.

Ann Cameron Mouat was now a very old lady, but had become increasingly dictatorial with the years, and was notorious for her refusal to pay for any repairs to any property, including her own house, Gardie House. Zachary was used to accommodating her many foibles ("I saw Aunt Ann on Monday, and I *think* she means to go south. She *locks* up the house when she is away so work must be done when she is at home..." he wrote in 1896). He had a long struggle to fund repairs to the Uyeasound shop, turning as usual to his cousin for assistance.

In March 1899 he wrote to Rev. Cameron:

I am glad you agree to do something to improve the shop. It really has much need. I am sure Aunt Ann won't object to anything you do so long as you don't ask her to contribute to the cost – but I do not see how you can reasonably be expected to do anything until the liferent held by Aunt Ann ceases. You cannot be expected to lay out money on property on which you are at present reaping no benefit.

Zachary eventually took the necessary decisions himself: "...probably Aunt Ann won't be pleased but the repairs are really necessary."

In 1899 Zachary took over the farm at Belmont in Unst and moved with his family into the house there. Some twenty years previously Belmont had been leased to Aunt Ann by her brother Major Cameron, along with other lands in Unst, for a nominal rent of 1/- per annum. The agreement carried an obligation "to keep and maintain the mansion house, offices and gardens in constant and proper repair." Not only had she not done so, but her tenant on the farm, John Jaffrey, had been "even more negligent with regard to his dykes, many of which were in a very ruinous condition" (Rev Cameron April 1900).

Upon his arrival at Belmont Zachary, with characteristic energy, set about putting things to rights with the farm and with the house, which, amongst other deficiencies, had no water supply. He decided to finance the repairs himself, remembering that "when my father came to Bressay there was no water and he laid it on at his own expense without costing the heritors anything." He made sure of his new water supply by installing an enormous cold water tank, 10 ft long, in the roof of the new extension to Belmont House.

Zachary Macaulay Hamilton.
© Macaulay Hamilton

In February 1900, however, Aunt Ann died at the Tingwall manse where she had latterly been looked after by her niece May Bayne, wife of the minister there. Her burial at Lund in Unst coincided with the great gale of that year.

Writing from his home at Belmont, Zachary described the event in a letter to Rev. Cameron dated 18 February:

On Wednesday we took the coffin to St Magnus at 5 am. Mr Bromley met us at the door and had a very short but nice service. On Thursday we had a service in St Magnus at 9 am and at 9.30 we removed the remains to the "Earl"[3] which started at 10. ... we got here at 2 pm. At that time it was blowing a flying gale, and the boats I had ordered to come round from Snarravoe could not get here although they had tried it twice. I had also ordered a flit boat from Cullivoe, fortunately they had come at 9 am with the last of the south tide and anchored in the bay. The steamer let go both anchors and fortunately held on and the Cullivoe boat got alongside. We got the remains, May, Mr Bayne, Lizzie and myself into the boat and with much difficulty got ashore, some of the men being to the neck in the water.

I had taken a hearse up and after we got ashore the boat attempted to go back to the "Earl" for the hearse, but it was blowing so hard they could not manage it and they had to let go their anchor to prevent their going on the rocks. We then got down a small boat and got the men out of the flit boat.... The "Earl" when she saw that the boat could not get to them again left and I believe went into Midyell where she must have remained until today.

Friday was the worst day I ever saw in my life and men of eighty say they never saw anything like it – a flying tempest and blinding snow and the sea fearful. The sea came right up through Moulla and carried away a large portion of my hay park dyke and a lot of sheep. At Uyeasound both the flit boats were smashed to matchwood. At Baltasound all Sandison's vessels (5) came ashore. The "Diana" their yacht was completely wrecked. The "Thomas Henry" a smack of 95 tons owned by Mr L Sandison and myself and which we had sold a fortnight ago to Swedes who came for her last week and were on board came ashore and tore her bottom out. Most of the fish curing stages are down and two of Mr Sandison's big herring boats that were hauled up were blown over and knocked to pieces. The damage about Baltasound alone will be several thousand pounds.

Saturday was little better than Friday. The funeral was to have been at noon but not a soul came. In fact I did not expect any. The drift is awful, all telegraph communication is stopped, almost all the telegraph poles between here and Baltasound are down, some broken at the ground, others halfway up, and poles and wires in one tangle across the road.

Today is a little better though still very bad. I have sent word to the men of Uyeasound and the Westing that the funeral will be at noon tomorrow weather permitting. Today between showers we can see a large ship ashore on the north end of Fetlar. I think the crew would be able to save themselves there as there is a little shelter where she is lying..."

The men who fought their way through the snow to Belmont carried the coffin to Lund for committal, a considerable feat, marked by stops for rest and refreshment[4].

Ann Cameron Mouat, the last of her siblings, was laid to rest in the family plot in the ancient kirk. The burial safely accomplished and the weather abated, Zachary went down to Bressay – where he was relieved to find storm damage not nearly so bad as he had feared – to take a look at Gardie House and safeguard any valuables. He found "a number of most interesting papers... from an antiquarian point of view most interesting and valuable..."; but the house itself, he was troubled to find, was badly in need of attention. It transpired that Aunt Ann had left the moveables to her niece May Bayne, who offered to sell the furniture at valuation to the long suffering Rev Cameron, and expressed the belief that the family portraits should most decidedly be his; but much of the beautiful family linen disappeared for ever.

Gardie House itself bore testimony to what happens to old Shetland houses when ongoing repairs are not carried out. Zachary reported endless defects, from serious woodworm infestation throughout to the dangerous state of the massive chimney stacks, 20 ft tall, where whole divisions were "completely decayed away," so that it was "a wonder the roof had not taken fire". In fact the roof was probably saved by the dampness of the whole building. "In a few years," he concluded, "it will be necessary to lay out a considerable sum on repairs."

These reports, plus the equally alarming ones on the state of Belmont, came to the Camerons at Ryde. Belmont was now in the capable hands of Zachary, but Gardie, that "bright, pleasant place", as Mary Cameron had described it in 1893, was a different matter.

The Camerons decided to carry out essential repairs to enable the house to be let, and financed the project by selling the Muness lands. It proved difficult, however, to get suitable workmen. "I am sorry to say there is not a joiner on the whole estate," wrote Zachary in April 1905. "In Bressay there are masons ... of course I always employ tenants as far as possible. I only know of one man in Shetland that would be suitable as he can do, and do well, joiner, plumber, slater and cement work ..."

Finally the Rev Cameron solved the problem by employing both an architect and a builder. His architect was from Edinburgh – John Bryce, nephew of David Bryce, the pivotal figure in the nineteenth century improvement and enlargement of many Scottish country houses, including Balfour Castle in Orkney. Bryce's ideas tended to the large and expensive, but he was checked both by distance, being unable to make other than occasional visits to Shetland, and also by the local builder, John Aitken.

Aitken was a highly successful builder with a string of commissions to his credit, including the Bass Rock and Sule Skerry lighthouses, and some of the more confident expressions of Lerwegian self-esteem, the Town Hall of 1882 and the Central School of 1902. He was technically extremely competent and possessed of common sense; the works he carried out in Gardie House were in the nick of time to save it from ruin and to modernise it for the new century.

There was a polite but keen series of disagreements between architect and builder in which Aitken generally came off the better, mostly because Bryce's proposals were expensive and the Camerons' basic idea, like house owners before and since, was to limit the expense and merely get the house weather proof, and habitable for the summers that they would be in residence (the idea of letting Gardie House died a quick death). This ensured that the house retained its original design.

Bryce's suggestion of raising the drawing room ceiling (which would have ruined its perfect proportions) and fitting glass doors to the china press in the panelling were rejected, but it was he who realised that the only way to safeguard the drooping floors (the drawing room floor was two inches lower at one end) was to use steel beams; and he also restored the original five windows to the drawing room by removing the shuttering which had obscured the end two in the dubious hope of increasing the warmth of the room.

Aitken's workmen uncovered many of the house's original features – an oven and separate chimney by the great fireplace in the hall; built drains under the ground floor, which, since they had never been cleared or repaired, were a source of smell and dampness; and the vast roof space, open for two centuries to the roof sarking save for two small partitioned off areas. This whole area was now clad with lath and plaster

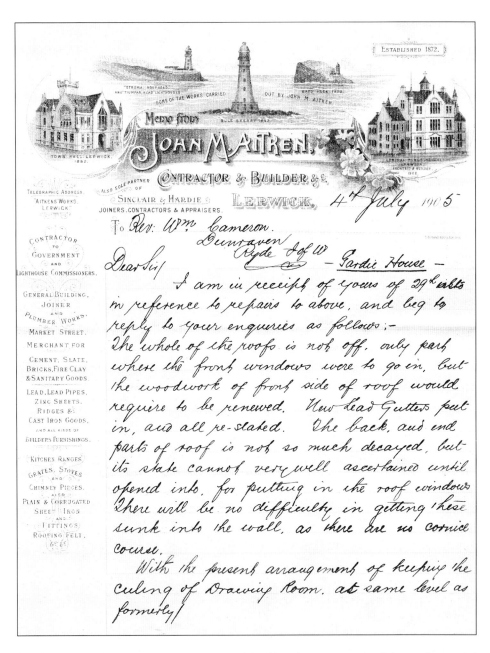

ESTABLISHED 1872.

Memo from

JOHN M. AITKEN.

CONTRACTOR & BUILDER &c.

ALSO SOLE PARTNER OF

SINCLAIR & HARDIE

JOINERS, CONTRACTORS & APPRAISERS.

LERWICK, 4th July 1905

TELEGRAPHIC ADDRESS,
"AITKENS WORKS,
LERWICK"

CONTRACTOR
TO
GOVERNMENT
AND
LIGHTHOUSE COMMISSIONERS.

GENERAL BUILDING,
JOINER
AND
PLUMBER WORKS,
MARKET STREET.

MERCHANT FOR

CEMENT, SLATE,
BRICKS, FIRE CLAY
& SANITARY GOODS.

LEAD, LEAD PIPES,
ZINC SHEETS,
RIDGES &
CAST IRON GOODS,
AND ALL KINDS OF
BUILDERS FURNISHINGS.

KITCHEN RANGES,
GRATES, STOVES
AND
CHIMNEY PIECES,
ALSO
PLAIN & CORRUGATED
SHEET IRON
AND
FITTINGS,
ROOFING FELT,
&c &c

To Rev: Wm. Cameron.
Dunraven
Ryde I of W — Gardie House —

Dear Sir

I am in receipt of yours of 29th ult.
in reference to repairs to above, and beg to
reply to your enquiries as follows;—
The whole of the roofs is not off, only part
where the front windows were to go in, but
the woodwork of front side of roof would
require to be renewed. New Lead Gutters put
in, and all re-slated. The back, and end
parts of roof is not so much decayed, but
its state cannot very well ascertained until
opened into, for putting in the roof windows
There will be no difficulty in getting these
sunk into the wall, as there are no cornice
course.

With the present arrangement of keeping the
Ceiling of Drawing Room, at same level as
formerly

The letterhead of J. M. Aitken, contractor and builder, depicting some of the works carried out by him, 4th July, 1905.

156

to create a series of bedrooms, which in its turn necessitated the raising of the front façade to accommodate proper windows. A bathroom and lavatory were also installed, and a hot water system.

The repairs to Gardie House illustrate perfectly the maxim, familiar to all who look after old buildings, that one thing leads to another. They took longer and cost more than had been anticipated, but, like William Mouat's works nearly 100 years previously, they lasted. The cement harl which finished the works remained intact until the 1970's rock blasting by Zetland County Council at Maryfield.

It might be supposed that, with the house now dryer, lighter and, by contemporary standards, enjoying modern amenities, that Shetland would exert a greater pull on the Camerons. They came up for summer visits with their two sons. The reactions of the older, Ewan, are not recorded, although it is likely that his easy manner and friendliness made a good enough impression. His shy younger brother, Norman, seven years Ewan's junior and very much in his shadow, flourished in Shetland, his health improving – he was a slave to asthma – and an interest in boats and the sea fostered by his surroundings. Norman was among those who watched enthralled as, with the roof repairs nearing completion, the big Edwardian wardrobes and the cast iron bath were hoisted up, since they could not be got up the circular stone staircase, to be lowered through the roof space and installed in the new rooms on the now habitable top floor of Gardie House.

With a child's perception too Norman picked up the story of the Swedish maid who had to be sacked for her habits of entertaining local men by letting down the ladder to her little bedroom in the tower of the old byre; a scandal which the adults carefully attempted to keep from the impressionable young, in which endeavour they inevitably failed.

Whatever the feelings of the rest of the family, its youngest member embarked with reluctance on the steamer to go south at the end of the holidays.

The truth seems to be that the works at Gardie House were probably simply another attempt by the Rev Cameron to do the right thing by his Shetland property.

He himself believed that his life's purpose was in the mission field, from which duty to wife and family had impelled him to withdraw. Discreet overtures were now coming his way from the Anglican Church

The entrance to Aberdeen harbour, 1882. (Drawing by M. A. Cameron).

in South Africa, well aware of the calibre of the man to whom they had so reluctantly bidden farewell twelve years previously.

In 1901 Rev Cameron allowed himself to be nominated for the post of Bishop of St John's Kafraria, the diocese where his church career had begun; this he did not do without much heartsearching and a careful review of the effects on his wife and family. The boys were growing up and away at school; his wife could be relied upon where their welfare was concerned; as for the marriage, the separation would be acceptable to both parties. He tried to think out all the options, finding, as he always had done, that he could confide in his sister Margaret, herself a seasoned traveller in Africa and now an Anglican nun.

> I have gradually been drawing to the idea that it might be well to free myself and my children from the responsibilities of the Shetland property, which I feel more and more that I cannot, with the other and higher claims upon me, properly discharge, and which might be a great encumbrance to Ewan, whose decided abilities seem to open out to him a future of great promise in a wider field than Shetland offers. (July 1901).

In the event the South Africa bishopric went to another; but psychologically the die was cast. It was now only a question of time.

For Cameron himself, the parish of Ryde, although conscientiously served, was hardly a satisfying outlet for his ability and energy, though it had certainly had its moments of interest. In December 1897 he had, by royal command, officiated at Divine Worship in the private chapel at Osbourne; in February 1900 he received an invitation to dine.

A dinner invitation from Queen Victoria was of course a command, as he pointed out when describing the event to his mother, and it necessitated Court dress, so that he had hastily to acquire knee breeches and silk stockings (his tailor in Ryde had to telegraph to London for the latter). He arrived by carriage in the snow, and was shown into a large drawingroom with a warming wood fire, where he was presently joined by the ladies and gentlemen of the Household, most of whom he had met before.

> About 9 or ½ past 9 someone said "The Queen", and I was told to go and stand near the door, behind the Lady in Waiting and the Maid of Honour, which I did, and made my bow when the Queen appeared in the corridor outside...then the Queen and Princesses went straight to the diningroom... and we all... went quickly to our places so as not to keep the Queen standing... then the Queen looked round the table, which was a signal to me to say grace, and we all sat down...I was the only guest... the dinner was an excellent one, consisting of 2 soups, 2 fish dishes, one or two entrees, meat, vegetable, game, sweets, cheese and dessert, but I have not the least idea of what many of the dishes were. Of course one was not obliged to eat everything, and there was no menu near me. Wines and mineral waters were handed; I don't think the Queen took any wine. Many of the plates seemed to be of silver... some of the dessert knives or forks seemed to be gold or gilt.... There were two Indians in native dress waiting, two or more Scotchmen in kilts, and footmen in scarlet livery... ... the gentlemen looked very grand with their ribbons and orders and medals..
>
> After dessert we all rose, the Queen led the way, supported by an Indian attendant, to the drawingroom .. after dinner coffee, liqueurs, and some coloured drinks, perhaps raspberry vinegar,... were handed round...presently.. the Master of the House was sent to call me..I went up to the Queen, and was rather reminded of going up to the Headmaster at school to have Latin verses looked over. As the Queen was sitting, I had to stoop a good deal to enable her to hear distinctly, as she does not like one to speak too loud. She asked ... what part of Scotland I came from, and about South Africa. I told her about Dalindyebo, my old pupil at Umtata, and how his father, the chief Ngargeligwe, used to call him "Prince of Wales", which seemed to amuse her. I also apologised for

having nearly run her down a few days before on my bicycle on my way to write my name in her book after preaching, as I passed an open gate just as she, most unexpectedly for me, was coming out in her donkey-chair, with no one in front of her. She seemed to be amused at that also... a little before eleven .. the Indian attendant came in and helped [the Queen] out, followed by the Princesses, while we all bowed... the Master of the Household then invited me and the other gentlemen... to come to one of the billiardrooms to smoke. Drinks were also offered... but we all thought it time to be getting home ...

This event caused much interest at home, but it hardly deflected Rev. Cameron from his chosen course. In 1902 the South African bishops asked him to come out "for a year or two" to undertake missionary training; a temporary post which he decided to accept. In the event he was away for 18 months, returning just in time to visit his mother before her death in January 1904, and to attend her funeral.

In December 1905 Zachary died suddenly of pneumonia at Belmont, aged only 50 and leaving a widow and three children, the youngest an infant of only two weeks. Once again the Rev Cameron refrained from taking the irrevocable step of selling his Shetland property. Instead he appointed as factor in Zachary's place William Gordon, who had recently come to live at Windhouse in Yell to take up sheep farming. Gordon was well qualified for the post, having been a solicitor for twenty years and handled the legal work for some of the big Angus estates, including the Earl of Home; he could safely be left to look after Garth in conjunction with the solicitors Blair and Cadell.

In the summer of 1906 Rev. Cameron visited Shetland where, as was his custom, he called upon every house on his estate; he also inspected the building works at Gardie House. He was alone, his wife and children not accompanying him; it was a business visit, with the aim of leaving things as well organised as possible, and it was the definitive break. In January 1907 he sailed for the Cape. There he was elected Coadjutor Bishop of Capetown.

In October 1910 Bishop Cameron's elder son, Ewan, celebrated his 21st birthday at Oxford, where he was an undergraduate. That summer his parents had given a party at Gardie House to mark the occasion: all the Bressay tenants and their families were invited and there was a dance in the local hall that evening.[5] Ewan was presented with a clock "From the people of Bressay" ; splendidly enamelled and suitably inscribed, it was

Bishop Cameron at his enthronement, 1907.

enthroned on the diningroom mantelpiece at Gardie House, where its chimes marked the passing of an age. (It is still there.)

Late the following year Ewan fell seriously ill. The doctors could not make a firm diagnosis, and the devoted care of his mother was not sufficient. "What the disease was that carried him off," wrote the Warden of New College later, "the doctors seem even yet not to be quite sure, but the fever had been upon him for many weeks, and has gradually sapped all his strength." Ewan died on 21st January, 1912, "an example of a pure, innocent, affectionate cheerful homeloving life, a good memory to cherish" added Dr Spooner with more prescience than he knew, "in these restless days".

Mrs Cameron's agony was borne alone; her younger son Norman, now 16, was at school and she wrote her husband not to return home. Bishop Cameron had received the news with a kind of religious rationalisation which enabled him to suppress grief "when I thought that 'God so loved the world, that he gave his only begotten son', I felt I could not grudge him mine, who after all is not my only son." (February 1912). The Bishop did come home the following year, when he followed his normal round of visits, church, family and Shetland. He had been back in Cape Town for nearly a year when war broke out in Europe in the summer of 1914.

Norman, now nearly old enough to leave school, wanted a career in the Army, a wish which persisted until in 1915 he was rejected on health grounds. Frustrated, Norman followed in Ewan's footsteps and became an undergraduate at Oxford, where he promptly reapplied for military

The clock presented to Ewan Cameron by the people of Bressay, 1910.

service. His mother, who had taken a house there to make a home for him, was only too aware of the situation. The appalling casualties on the Western front were beginning to penetrate British public consciousness. "I saw George Holland lately, looking very thin and worn and sad, no wonder when he has lost all his friends in his old regiment, only 3 officers left out of 28, and 200 men out of the full strength of 1000 or more...." wrote Mary Cameron early in 1915.

By now the army was desperate for men. In February 1915 Mary Cameron wrote to her sister-in-law in Shetland:

> This is only a brief line for you and Jeannie too... I am rather stunned by the rapid change of plans and the rush of events, and very tired... for Norman has gone – to Sandhurst – and his life here is at an end, just too when he seemed to be growing into [it]... with the doctor's leave he applied a few days ago for his commission and was told by the Vice Chancellor that as it was for a permanent one... it would mean Sandhurst and that being very full there might be delay. So we supposed that perhaps after the Easter holidays he might be admitted. But suddenly there came a telegram from the War Office nominating him to Sandhurst and telling him to be there within two days, so he had to pack hastily... and left yesterday...
>
> It means the front, for he has given his choice as the Cameron Highlanders, and that has been out from the beginning and has suffered severely (one poor young cousin who has been "wounded and missing" since early September was in that, a boy of 20 and an only son...)... they may keep him 2 or 3 months at Sandhurst, but it depends on fitness and on the urgent needs of the regiments...

> Quite three fourths of the undergraduates have gone from here and many of the younger dons too, with of course temporary commissions, alas! very temporary indeed already many of them. Of the Oxford "territorials" gone out I believe only 2 have survived. It is a terrible time, and no one pretends now not to look grave...

Norman's time at Sandhurst was to be brief; the needs of the army were urgent indeed. Perhaps fortunately, his father underestimated the speed with which young officers made the transition from civilian life to front line.

Meanwhile the Bishop himself was also in khaki, at least briefly, when he travelled up the coast in a hospital ship as the campaign against German South West Africa took shape; he witnessed its aftermath. "... the natives had a very bad time under the Germans... in the southern part, which we have now taken, [they] were pretty well exterminated." (2 July 1915). His church duties now included visiting wounded men and bereaved families. He had no settled home, often living in campaign conditions, and when in Capetown merely renting rooms in Church House; under these pressures, his health began to break down.

He died in November 1915, from post-operative peritonitis, a week past his 61st birthday. His wife wrote: "... it is as he would have wished in the country that was most home to him". Inevitably, when the telegram arrived, she had feared for another. "I am glad (the Bishop) was spared the anxiety of knowing Norman is in the trenches," she wrote to her sister-in-law; "... of course when the telegram came I thought it was about Norman..."

South African newspapers recorded Bishop Cameron's passing and praised his dedication to the peoples of that country; elsewhere, amidst the greater slaughter, it went mostly unnoticed. Norman was now on the front line, where the life expectancy of a subaltern was reckoned at three weeks.

NOTES:

1   Hoggs – ewe lambs of previous spring.
2   yield: year-old sheep.
3   *Earl of Zetland* – the steamer which served the north isles of Shetland.
4   George Jamieson, Uyeasound, Unst, pers com.
5   The late Mrs Mary Smith, Cruetown, Bressay, pers com.

CHAPTER EIGHT

THE TWENTIETH CENTURY

I'm very touched to hear that some people asked after me after all this time ... Mrs Mary Inkster lived at Gardie, Uyeasound, and knitted lovely cardigans for me. But they were all wonderful people ... in fact my years in Shetland were the happiest time of my life.
Mary MacDonnell, Canberra, Australia, to author, December 1992.

In early 1916 the new owner of the Garth estate in Shetland, Norman Ogilvie Mouat Cameron, who had just celebrated his 20th birthday, was posted to the 1st Battalion Cameron Highlanders, then stationed on the front line in the mining area of Loos, where they had previously suffered heavy casualties. They were then moved south towards the Somme, where the next big push was planned. The battle itself took place in July, and it was there that he received the wounds which probably ensured that he survived the war.

His injuries left him semi-disabled. Thanks to the care of the famous orthopaedic surgeon Sir Robert Jones his foot was saved, but his general health never fully recovered. By September 1916 he was on crutches, although "very thin and worn, and has not much strength", as his mother wrote to the family in Shetland. Just over a year later Cameron himself wrote from army camp at Wendover. After a naval engagement between Norway and Shetland in which two British destroyers were sunk, he thought it possible that "they may come nearer next time, and if they

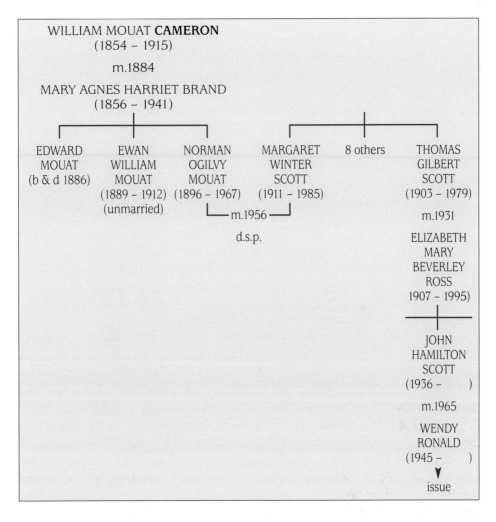

WILLIAM MOUAT **CAMERON**
(1854 – 1915)

m.1884

MARY AGNES HARRIET BRAND
(1856 – 1941)

| EDWARD MOUAT (b & d 1886) | EWAN WILLIAM MOUAT (1889 – 1912) (unmarried) | NORMAN OGILVY MOUAT (1896 – 1967) | MARGARET WINTER SCOTT (1911 – 1985) | 8 others | THOMAS GILBERT SCOTT (1903 – 1979) |

— m.1956 —

d.s.p.

THOMAS GILBERT SCOTT
m.1931

ELIZABETH MARY BEVERLEY ROSS
1907 – 1995)

JOHN HAMILTON SCOTT
(1936 –   )

m.1965

WENDY RONALD
(1945 –   )

▼
issue

by any chance land a shell on the property, I particularly should like the spot left as it is ... a shell hole in Shetland will be a rare curiosity, and worth preserving ..." (a comment also showing the gulf between the men at the front and the civilians who knew so little of what was happening).

He was back in France by the summer of 1918. After the Armistice he served with his Battalion, now part of the occupying force in Germany, but had to be invalided home. He left the army for the Reserve of Officers, and resumed his interrupted studies at Oxford. There he took the shortened course prescribed for those whose time had been constricted by the war, and gained a Distinction in the Honours School of Modern History. He also took the Civil Service exam, passed high in the list, and secured his first preference, a place in the Department of Printed Books, British Museum.

Now in his early twenties, Norman Cameron, like the other survivors of his generation, tried to put the past behind him. In London he soon found friends and interests; he was one of the founders of the English Country Dance Society, and his love of music, in particular opera, soon resulted in regular reviewing for the *Gramophone* magazine.

His life and interests lay far from Shetland; but he retained a strong affection for the islands and, with his mother, came up every summer, often bringing a party of friends. Gardie House came to life again, staffed with local women to cook and clean. The house was Spartan: one young employee later recalled how she put her gloves on when she went up to make the beds on the top floor.[1] Cameron could now indulge his passion for the sea; he acquired two boats, named *Casilda* and *Iolanthe* for characters in his favourite Gilbert and Sullivan operas.

There seemed no reason why this pattern should not continue indefinitely. But London in the 1920s with its smogs and dirty air took its toll on his fragile health; his chest condition worsened to the point where, in a repetition of his own father's health crisis, he was told by his doctors that he must live in an unpolluted climate. For Norman Cameron there could only be one option. In 1929 he returned to live permanently in Shetland.

Shetland between the wars was not immune from the economic woes general throughout Britain. The island economy remained dependent upon fish, livestock and hosiery[2]. The crofting communities, fixed into a rigid pattern, found adaptation difficult; emigration was one answer, fostered, too, by the wholesale shake-up of ideas and attitudes which is one of the by-products of war. The small size of Shetland crofts brought the need for more grazing land into sharp focus. Hence a stream of complaints to the estate, all founded on the inability of crofts to afford their occupants a proper living.

Thus in March 1914 the tenants of Beosetter complained about their neighbour George Sutherland of Gunnista, whose sheep "are jumping into our cabbage yards which our animals and ourselves are depending on for food. We have told him about it more than once and he pays no heed to us ..." And several groups of tenants wrote to ask that the scattald be rented to them: "it would make our lot much easier," commented the Norwick and Valsgarth tenants in north Unst, "as we have always been badly hampered for want of sufficient grazing for our animals, and now especially with the need for output so great, to meet the increased cost of living, we find it increasingly difficult to carry on without more grazing land ..."

Pre-eminent in this move was Laurence Laurenson, later the first chairman of the new Grazings Committee, who was an estate tenant for seventy-seven years, a record unlikely ever to be surpassed. Laurenson himself was party to one of the several disputes where newly constituted committees tried to enforce stocking levels on these easily exhausted grazings, only to find individuals ignoring them. Hence the difficulty with the Hamar Skaw lands in north Unst where it was considered that the land should carry cattle only during the summer months; a similar problem arose in the Easting in south Unst.

Other disputes concerned difficult neighbours, like the Mrs Johnson at Heogan in Bressay who "proved a source of trouble with her sheep and horses since she came to this district and annoyed the peace of the neighbours who have lived in peace all their lives", as Alan Roy the factor was informed by James Cooper, Jane Smith and Maggie White (March 1929).

Another letter (August 1916) from the residents of South Bressay suggests the feeling which could be engendered:

> We hereby inform you, that Laurence Laurenson of Hillside Bressay has taken away the cart gate through which we all had to cart our peats, and put in its place a small one which a cart cannot pass through. The gate which he has taken away has been used for a cart gate as long as any of us can remember, and why should Laurence Laurenson be allowed to take away this gate when he had no authority to do so. Take for instance poor old George Smith who is lying dying and his daughter who has enough to do to attend him and cannot get a few peats down from the hill, and all through this black-hearted trick of Laurence Laurenson's. I hope sir as you are a gentleman you will do to your utmost, in getting him to replace the gate which he took away, as quickly as possible as the winter will soon be close at hand.

Garth Estate tenants, who had for a generation no resident proprietor, found presently they had one again, but one who continued to delegate administrative functions to a factor. In 1918 this post was filled

Allan Roy and Henry Williamson outside the Uyeasound shop, April 1935.

by Allan Roy, surveyor and land valuer, who lived at Helendale in Lerwick. Roy worked with the estate ground officer Henry Williamson, of the Westing in Unst, and their partnership, which rapidly developed into friendship, was to last for twenty years.

Williamson owned his own croft; capable and energetic, he had lived all his life in Unst and had therefore a close knowledge of the folk and how they behaved, not just on the croft but in other ways too. His letters, forthright, unsentimental, and practical, paint a picture of life in the North Isles as vivid in their way as those written by Zachary Macaulay Hamilton a generation earlier. Williamson wrote as he spoke – although his letters are in English, and lack the self-conscious orthography of much written Shetland dialect, the phraseology and cadences are unmistakeable: "I think you should give him your best consideration as his father has no land and he is brought up a large family on nothing except what he is gotten from the sea and now he is getting to be an old man ..."

As Williamson got to know Roy his opinions, frank as they were, went down on paper. In February 1920 he wrote:

> Polson is giving up the shop at Uyeasound, I think the Sandisons is taking over his stock. His sister is getting married and his wife will not stop, she told me that the house does not suit her and a lot more of reasons but I doubt they will not tell the real reason, for he was never made to be a merchant.

And later:

> I am having a bad time with D Fraser's sheep, he will not keep them off Snaborough. They bolt through his fence like rabbits ... if I would speak to him I would get nothing but unreason.

About people he became more outspoken as his confidence in Roy increased. In March 1921 he described an incident at Snarravoe:

> Robert Ray (a tenant of yours at Snarravoe) and his mother went amissing on Monday night. She was found dead lying under a dyke on Friday morning but no trace is of him as yet and if ever he is found he will be dead. They have no near heir and they are left plenty after them but there is one man in the house. The police is taken charge. I told him he would have to pay the rent in full or pay ½ and give up all claims. There would be no fear in him getting the other half for grazing.
>
> "No doubt you will be getting offers for the croft for extensions but excuse me you should not be in a hurry to let it until you know the parties as there has been friction there before...

Roy evidently did as he was advised as it was that autumn before Williamson again wrote:

> "... when [at Belmont] I spoke with John Cluness he asked if I knew where you were, I asked him what was the matter. He said he wrote you asking if he could get Ray's place at Snarravoe but he was got no word as yet. I said to him are you truly wanting the place and he said that he was anxious to get it for his son, the teacher put it in his mind, and that you need not fear about the rent as his sons would see to that as they were done before.
>
> Then I said to him what are you going to do about the croft you hold at Meal that J P Sandison is occupying, he said that he would give up that place if you would give him Snarravoe. Now the Williamsons wants the place and the Sutherlands also wants it, and by giving it to Cluness would put all things right and it is a pity to see a house going down when a man wants to live in it. The Sutherlands is ruined one house so they should not get another to ruin ... regarding the place at Snarravoe I cannot think it should be raised in rent, it was always the cheapest rent in olden times and was also considered the worst and I now see for myself that it is. I see by Mr Sangster that he would like the Sutherlands to get it, but they have too much already, and Cluness is an ex-Service man, what they are not, they were all shirkers."

In 1923 he described a February gale:

> I went over to Norwick to see what was up. The sea with the gale is
> wrought terrible work with the beach at Norwick, it is taken away about
> 180 yards of dykes belonging to L Laurenson and Ellen Henderson, it is
> also covered more than an acre of their cultivated land with stones and
> a whole lot of their grass is covered with land. The burn is also closed up
> so that the water is up the valley like a loch. It will take a great deal of
> labour to make things anything like right again.
>
> They are looking to you for either a reduction of rent or help to
> remove the beach off the land and build dykes, also to open the burn. ..
> it is a big job (the sea took Andrew Gray and he was nearly away with it).

Williamson's world was one where poverty was widespread. Much
housing stock was of poor quality ("with regard to the enclosed letter I
was in said house in spring, it is a very miserable house, the walls is just
like a dyke and it has a thatched roof with earth floor and it looked to me
that water is coming in everywhere. My opinion is that it wants a new
roof and the walls pointed ..." December 1924). The poorhouse was the
final home of more than one elderly person, and disease wreaked its toll
– in 1929 an outbreak of scarlet fever in Unst caused several deaths,
including a mother and child. Agriculture limped along, with poor prices
and a worldwide depression in the 1930s bad enough to leave farms
untenanted as confidence plummeted.

In 1929 the Board of Agriculture proposed to break up the farm of
Uyeasound and re-establish the four small crofts on the land. Roy wrote
Williamson: "I would very much like if you could get me estate tenants
who are requiring holdings so that I can put forward my proposals as to
suitable tenants requiring land ..."

By now Roy was accustomed to a frank sharing of information:

> Laurence Niven is very much annoyed with me for telling him a few
> home truths regarding his method of getting land from the Department.
> The Board offered him a small rig at Vatchlees and I wished to get him a
> better and larger piece of land, but he thought he was much more clever
> than I so he has signed for the small piece and I have taken his name off
> from the larger, he now thinks I should send him an apology, what next
> I wonder.

Landlords no longer had to deal with tenants' disputes, a role which
now fell to the Land Court. This was enthusiastically embraced in certain
parts of the estate.

170

In July 1929 the tenants of Norwick in Unst awaited the arrival of the Land Court to resolve what Roy considered "their various troubles and family quarrels. Life for them would not be worth living if they did not have the excitement of an imaginary grievance and the Land Court yearly." It did become almost an anuual event.

In May 1932 Roy wrote:

> ... we are going to have plenty cases from Norwick this year before the Land Court. They all seem to have fallen out among themselves. Its possibly the best thing that could happen at this time as it should keep them quiet for some years after they get their various decisions.

Williamson commented in reply "... you or no-one will ever get that people satisfied, they must have something to talk about". It eventually transpired that the trouble seemed to be caused by Laurence Laurenson putting a new gate on the cliff path. "This being from Norwick," sighed Roy, "I am never very sure if their complaints are not really family quarrels."

It certainly came as no surprise when the route of the projected new road also caused fierce disputes and the fate of the gate or gates on the cliff path – Williamson went up to see for himself and reported that there had been a gate before and there were now two – gave all concerned plenty of mind-occupying activity until solutions were arrived at. Altogether Roy seems to have come to accept Williamson's approach to the disputes which formed an integral part of community life: "... there seems to be faults on both sides in connection with Messrs Mouat and Smith's dispute and possibly your suggestion to meanwhile leave them to it, is the better plan."

But disputes were not confined to the rural scene. The Church of Scotland distinguished itself in post-war, poverty-stricken Shetland, by making demands "out of all reason" for repairs due on ecclesiastical buildings. The heritors were "not to be allowed to repair the buildings themselves"; so in self-defence, and finding the Church's General Trustees "asking so outrageous figures", they instigated a Shetland-wide protest.

"The Trustees would think twice," wrote Roy, as he circulated the various parishes, "when they were aware a whole county was in arms against their demands and might be more amenable to reason." (November 1927).

This incident probably helps to explain Williamson's comment several years later: "... what is up with the Church that they are selling the Glebe, I think that all the Ministers should be disposed of likeways". Roy agreed. "I quite agree with you that the ministers should be disposed of as well as the glebes, but I'm afraid the glebes would fetch in the most money."

This anti-clericalism was shared by their employer. Norman Cameron, in writing to Mr Cadell, had "referred to my recent gift, under compulsion, of £1000 to St Magnus Church. This seems to have alarmed him ... I suppose he understood I had given another £1000, whereas I of course meant my Aunt's legacy. As if I would go giving anything to any religious body !"

His writing style already showed the terse wittiness he never achieved personally, which in later years had the secretaries in the office of his Edinburgh lawyer diving to open the envelopes with their unmistakeable green typewriter ink: "... had a visit from Tulloch (small, spectacled, unshaved, whom I remember seeing before), wanting croft ... I told him to put it in writing, but he has not yet... " (1929).

Meanwhile Henry Williamson was ageing: "I have been in bed since I wrote you last, but I got out yesterday, the weather is so cold and bad up here that I thought it best to stop in bed as I could not get out." He was no longer able to travel to Lerwick where he had formerly enjoyed a night out with Roy at Up-Helly-A', and getting about on his bicycle, his normal method of travel, became increasingly arduous. Roy's concern took the practical form of insisting that Williamson should hire a car to drive him wherever when he had to go on estate business. In January 1938 Roy was incapacitated by a stroke; he was hospitalised in Ballater where he died a few months later. Williamson himself died in November that same year.

So it was that as war loomed, the estate was deprived of knowledgeable administrators, and about to lose its owner once again, for it was clear that Norman Cameron would immediately volunteer for active service. For the past ten years he had lived in Shetland, but, although he could express himself in writing, he was personally reserved, and had only to a limited extent settled into the community. Being the product of one particular type of upbringing, and essentially not a practical man in a society which was so very practical, he found it hard to get on terms with those whose experience was so different. His very strong love for Shetland remained, perhaps, unrealised by others. He had

The first aeroplane to land in Bressay, piloted by captain Fresson, in October 1933,
photographed beside the first car to arrive in Bressay, January 1933. The plane landed in the
Long Park. The Maryfield farm steading is to the rear, with its thorn hedge clearly visible.

been therefore thrown back upon his own resources to an undesirable extent. By the time he was 40 he had written his obituary.

In 1936 Lunna House was taken for the summer by the explorer Tom Longstaff, who brought his wife and seven daughters, and his niece Margaret Scott, who was contemporary with her elder nieces. The Longstaff girls had inherited their parents' verve – Longstaff himself had spent his life climbing in the Himalaya and had been on the 1922 Everest expedition, while his wife Dora Scott had the stamina for bringing up her large family without any husbandly assistance whilst remaining sane – and Norman Cameron found them fairly intimidating. But Meg Scott was different. Unassuming and lacking in self-confidence, but possessing both humour and intelligence, Meg had some characteristics in common with the shy laird of Bressay. Before she left again for the south, they were engaged.

By the autumn Cameron had travelled to the south of England to meet his fiancee's family. It was a large one – Meg was the youngest of ten children – and they extended a curious but warm welcome to the stranger from the north. The marriage followed in November 1936, from the bride's home in Bournemouth. She wore a lace veil lent by her sister-in-law Elizabeth, wife of Meg's favourite brother Tom. Elizabeth herself was unable to come to the wedding as she imminently expected the birth of her second baby.[3]

The newly-married pair returned to Shetland for Christmas 1936, after a honeymoon spent in the south of Italy, not entirely a comfortable choice since it coincided with the height of the Abyssinian crisis, involving both Britain and fascist Italy. The Camerons found it a relief to reach the pro-British sanctuary of Malta. For Meg her first winter in Shetland was a baptism of cold and damp – during January 1937 the wind never dropped below gale force and Gardie House lacked not only electricity but even a reliable water supply. But there were compensations, including unobtrusive kindness from the Bressay community, who gave as a wedding present two beautiful teak gates decorated with carved sailing ships.[4]

The arrival of Meg Cameron at Gardie House meant that for the first time in the history of the house, the distaff side of life had its chronicler. Most of her extant correspondence was to her husband, as war separated them, and the history of her home front is coupled with the personal history of a young woman (Meg was aged 24 when she married, 16 years younger than her husband) learning to cope in an unfamiliar environment.

In July 1937 she wrote:

> Yesterday was a morning of dense fog, so dense that I could scarcely see the garden gate. I daren't go across [to Lerwick] till it lifted a bit as the whole Sound seemed teeming with boats according to the noise they made. However it got better about noon ... earlier there was a collision immediately opposite the Fish Mart. A trawler and a Lerwick fishing boat, the kind with wooden sides, collided, and the fishing boat sank in three minutes. Today I see the place is well marked with buoys ... I've just got in after fishing all afternoon in Brough and catching nothing, in spite of old Tom Laurenson's advice ... on my way home I was overtaken by a party of trippers from Noss. I was walking slowly with all my gear and a fat man with a Yorkshire accent said to me, 'you'll have to walk faster if you want to catch the ferry'. 'It's all right,' I said, 'I live here.' 'Fancy that, ' he said to the others, 'and I can understand every word she says.'

*Mrs Cameron (Meg) visiting
Maggie Robina Gifford,
Flasgarth, Bressay, late 1930s.*

These quiet days soon gave way to the kind of preparations being made nationwide.

August 22, 1940:

> We went to Lerwick yesterday morning, did shopping, and brought back the man from Shearer's who has fixed the red curtains, and they really look rather imposing. Whether they are efficient in blacking out the staircase window I don't yet know, as I got in too late last night to experiment. He is also going to make a dark blind to fit the skylight over the back stairs. All this is a bore, but I do like to feel I can move about the house freely after dark ... this morning I have cleared out all the brooms, brushes and papers from under the backstairs, Annie[5] has scrubbed it out, and I have placed there two stools, two rugs, a cushion, a tin of biscuits, Hetty's first aid outfit, and my gas-mask. We will only go there if there is a really bad raid, but it looks quite cosy and almost inviting, rather like a cosy-corner for sitting out at a dance...

Like many another wife writing to an absent husband, she filled her pages with the small things.

> I blacked out the bathroom successfully yesterday, so I can light a candle ... a Spitfire fund has been started in Shetland ... I saw the pet lamb trot,

unnoticed, along the pier following Robertson this morning, and then it was just prevented in time from hurling itself into the boat after him.

Writing to her husband in Derby, a Luftwaffe target, that September:

> I think you would have much sympathy with Michael, who, when woken up in the middle of the night and told to get dressed and go to the shelter, remarked, 'this is just another lousy trick to get me out of bed' ... it gets dark much earlier now, and I shall soon have to light the candles for dinner. I light the lamps directly afterwards ... it has been pleasant and peaceful up here, and, though it is a relief to find I can manage to cope with the material business of living, such as lamps and parcels, without your help, I miss you too much to put up with unnecessary separation ...

The Camerons were reunited, briefly, in London that winter, when Meg came south to see her family. Norman Cameron's job as Movement Officer in Inverness fell far short of what he wished for. The army sent him on various courses and he applied for other jobs, but he was too old and not well enough for the kind of active duty he had – unrealistically – hoped for. In May 1940 he had to endure the personal bitterness of dealing with the young men who were doing the fighting, when he was in Perth to meet the troops coming home from Norway. He had home leave in the summer, but was back in Inverness by July, leaving his wife yet again to hold the fort at Gardie.

Meg was very lonely; but made friends with some of the service people and their wives, and her isolation must have become apparent to some, for that summer she was asked out in Lerwick to stay overnight, a thoughtful response to the difficulties of travel which were part of her situation.

One particularly happy excursion was to the Adies at Voe, when Mrs Adie cooked dinner:

> ... one of the best I've ever had ... first, cold boiled lobster and salad (home grown lettuce and tomatoes), then roast wild duck, apple sauce, home-grown spinach and potatoes, followed by a most glorious cold chocolate souffle and cream. Who would have thought there is a war on?... I didn't see Mrs Hamilton. She is very sad as she has just heard her youngest son is missing in Greece with the New Zealanders.[6]

Getting a car to Bressay. Norman Cameron's Austin 7 being conveyed to Bressay on the
Norna, *1935.*

A week later she had another outing, to Busta, where the tenant was
about to leave:

> Mrs White let us go all over the house ... I didn't realise it was so old. Most
> of it is 15th century, the drawingroom, which has panelling and two
> china presses like ours, being built out over the staircase in 1714 ... we
> went up to the garret, where poor Barbara Pitcairn is supposed to have
> had her baby[7], it was very dirty and I was horrified to see a lot of old
> leather-bound books and a lovely papier-mache table covered with dust
> and damp. We saw the portraits too, but they were bad, and Mrs White
> didn't know who was which. Nearly all the rooms are panelled, and the
> wood is thought to have come from wrecks. It is a very big house and
> could be made beautiful ...

That summer was a busy one.

> The brigadier is coming to lunch on Sunday ... I was a bit scared when
> he rang up to say he was coming and added 'I thought I'd let you know

... so you could kill the fatted calf for me.' I had previously thought of some simple wartime dish such as curried eggs, but now have ordered a lobster and a chicken ... I'm afraid you will get a large bill from Hay and Co for the coal, but we were lucky to get it before the rationing came in. It ought to last more than a year, I should think. I am still burning peat, eked out with drift wood, in the library.

On 21 July the Brigadier did come to lunch, and it was a great success:

> ... he calls me 'poor, peerie, peaty, widdie' because he thinks that must be Shetlandic for 'grass widow' ... Robina's brother, who painted our kitchen, has been given the BEM for helping the captain save his ship after she had been torpedoed. We have a nice lot of vegetables in the garden now. It was rather unfortunate about the radishes, which we had not grown before. Robertson, being unacquainted with them, singled them out like turnips till they were about a foot apart, thinking they would grow to an enormous size! ... I hear one of Molly's brothers is missing, she had five brothers all at sea. I wonder what's happened to a lot of people I haven't heard from since this war began ...

In August 1941 Meg left Shetland for the south of England, where she stayed with her widowed mother in Bournemouth. She and Norman spent his embarkation leave in London, after which she returned to Bournemouth, where she could get war work. With all the men away, there was a desperate demand for educated women to fill Civil Service posts. By November Meg was working in the War Savings Department.

Her letters to her husband went quite literally into the blue. News of him first reached her from Halifax, Nova Scotia, and subsequently Durban, South Africa, and it seems that he was still working in Movement Control, since these were strategic locations for convoys. But travel, stress and overwork took their toll. Early the following year, he was in Bombay, and his health had finally broken down. His mental anguish at not being able to play what he saw as an active part in the war effort was compounded by not receiving any of Meg's letters. At last, in March 1942, he finally returned to Britain.

As it seemed likely that he would be invalided out of the army Meg, "filled with joy", returned to Shetland in May in time to save Gardie House from being requisitioned by the army (they were satisfied with the adjacent, and vacant, house of Maryfield once it was pointed out to them).

Meg resumed the endless daily tasks which living at Gardie House entailed, and her reports to her husband. "The Brigadier has just acquired a luxury yacht, almost a liner, as well as his honkey-tonk. He keeps one here and the other at Scalloway. When the SNO (Senior Naval Officer) got a car, the brig said 'what do you want a car for?' so the SNO replied 'why do you keep a fleet?'"

She recounted the everyday difficulties of wartime life – fuel rationing – "I do not see how we could manage without peats" (though it was very difficult to find anyone to cut them); the arrangements to be made with emergency supplies lest blitzed army wives had to be housed at Gardie House; her bout of German measles that month; and the return of the faithful Jessie to back her up on the domestic front.

But she was desperately lonely. "I feel a bit mad at times, and often catch myself talking to myself." And the everyday demands of living in Gardie House took most of her time and energy: "more library books have come and I've only read a quarter of one of the previous batch! I don't get much time."

Meantime her letters to a husband she had not seen for nearly a year showed how, like so many other women, she had gained in confidence

MV Hilarion, *built by Sandisons of Baltasound for Norman Cameron in 1936. Sold after the war.*

by having to cope; and attempted to respond to the unhappiness which she recognised in his letters. In late June she told him – *"don't be so sad, Norman …we have much to be thankful for, more than a lot of people."*

But Norman Cameron had found his return to Britain hard to cope with; a sense of failure coupled disastrously with survivor's guilt untreated since the First War. In July 1942 he left the army and came home to live.

The post-war years saw the Camerons settled at Gardie House. There Norman Cameron put his abilities to the service of his estate. His legacy was two-fold: the paying off, after more than 100 years, of all the debts which encumbered it, accomplished, since rents were low and income spoken for, by a domestic regime of unremitting frugality; and the saving and sorting of the vast mass of family papers and other documents which were later to be codified as the Gardie House Archive.

Post-war Shetland saw a painfully gradual adjustment to modern living. The first tractor came to Bressay in 1948; a public electricity supply five years later. The 1950s were a difficult decade – agriculture, having revived during the war, slumped again, fishing remained underdeveloped, and the smaller islands like Bressay, lacking basic amenities like electricity, water and reasonable transport links, steadily lost population. People had seen for themselves that there were better chances elsewhere.

The Camerons, at Gardie House, childless and ageing, became increasingly isolated, and found themselves victimised by a politically extreme faction in local government. Annsbrae House in Lerwick was compulsorarily purchased by the Town Council to be demolished, from which act of gratuitous vandalism they were only restrained by the intervention of the Secretary of State for Scotland[8].

At about the same time the county council, publicly criticising Norman Cameron for his failure to improve the Uyeasound pier in Unst, demanded that it be handed over without compensation. The row dragged on until 1964, when the pier became the property of Zetland County Council. These two compulsory purchases, driven by political dogma, failed to benefit the people of Shetland. Annsbrae stood empty for twenty years, and the ZCC was never prepared to invest the monies required for significant improvement to the Uyeasound Pier, either for inter-island transport or, later, local salmon farmers.

It was after these two bruising episodes that Cameron wrote the codicil to his will in which he stipulated that if either Gardie House or Belmont fell into the hands of the local authority they were to be blown up.

In 1951 he engaged Mary MacDonnell to act as estate factor. Miss MacDonnell (she was christened 'Korea' by the Bressay folk), coming fresh to the islands, recorded somewhat happier impressions in a letter which is now a testimony to one facet of a Shetland which has disappeared.

In April 1951 she wrote an American friend, Gayle Raymond Kennedy:

> The estate I manage is scattered over the islands and comprises some thirty thousand acres. There are four big farms but otherwise it is all just bare hill or little plots of five or six acres. There are some two hundred tenants of these little plots, each with their little cottage and cowshed and a few sheep and sometimes a cow and some hens. They are very poor but very independent and can do most things for themselves. They are an attractive people, friendly, anxious to please, but very jealous of their independence and difficult to induce to act together for their common good. They regard me as a foreigner, of course, but because I am Irish they welcome me, because lots of Irish girls used to come here to work in the curing of herrings, and they liked them and got on well with them ... I have all the rents to collect (once a year), the accounts to do, a good deal of correspondence of one sort or another; I allot vacant tenancies and deal with legal questions. Outside I visit the tenants and see that they are keeping their fences, their houses, their stone walls, their farm buildings in repair; that they are keeping their drains clear, that they are cutting their peat in the right places and restoring the ground in the proper manner afterwards. I try to settle disputes and make the revenue keep up with the expenditure. It is fascinating and varied and never monotonous. I am my own master, more or less, because though my employer lives here he can't work up much interest in the estate, which is why he engaged me to run it for him. ... at the moment I live with my employer and his wife in a big eighteenth century house as spacious and elegant as it is glacially cold. They are kind and don't interfere with me, but they have reached a pitch of absorption in things of the intellect (they are both graduates of Oxford) where they are almost moribund. They are so divorced from the realities of life ...
>
> If you come to Europe again, will you come and stay with me? You travel to Aberdeen and then you board a steamer for the Shetland Isles one evening and the next morning you wake up and find you are there.

I will shew you a landscape without a single tree, but where the sea is hardly ever out of sight. I will shew you fishing boats, little toy fishing boats, but with motor engines nevertheless, racing in with the morning to sell their catch; black hulls with gay yellow band round the top and the number of the boat picked out in white and blue. They come dashing over a sea so blue you look twice to see if it is really as blue as you think; and the air is so clear that the colour of the crops on the land almost dazzles. The cottages snuggle into the sides of the hills and their black tarred roofs look Prussian blue in the sun. I'll shew you men cutting peat and stacking it in little card houses to dry in the wind and weeks later I'll shew you the same peats being carried in nets slung each side of a pony, and whole trains of twenty or thirty of these ponies being driven from the peat banks back to the cottages where the peat is built into a stack. I'll shew you gannets diving straight from a hundred feet up in the sky and coming up with a fish every time; I'll shew you cliffs rising two hundred feet sheer from the sea and every inch covered with nesting seabirds. Rows and rows of guillemots looking like dinner-jacketed gentlemen at boxes in the opera-house, clusters of little puffins looking like old men discussing politics ...

Here at the end of the world everything is more expensive because it costs so much to get it here – but it seems more valuable where there are few shops and those devoted to the necessities of life rather than the amenities. We have no theatre, no concerts, one cinema and rather poor radio reception ... communications are inclined to be hazardous, so one

The Swan *fishing smack, restored thanks to twentieth century oil wealth, and the island of Noss, now a National Nature Reserve managed by government scientists. But the image – a boat and an island – remains timeless.*

> relies mainly on oneself and one's books for entertainment. This makes
> a visit to the civilised south a tremendous event and one gobbles up art
> exhibitions, theatres, concerts, social life of whatever sort, in a
> gluttonous feast. In a way such contrasts seem to infuse a zest into life
> which it did not have when one lived in the midst of plenty.

In 1955 a new Crofters Act was passed, which removed most of the remaining functions of a landlord. All decisions were henceforth taken by the Crofters' Commission in Inverness, thus substituting rule by civil servants for any more locally based system.

The propensity of civil servants to do nothing in difficult situations resulted in a serious problem of absentee crofting tenants throughout the crofting counties. In vain did landlords protest against tenants who lived far from their crofts and the invidious system of subletting at will, an arrangement every bit as arbitrary as anything that had happened in the past.

There were also various schemes for reorganising holdings: in Shetland this happened in Fetlar. But it was not a success, and was not repeated elsewhere[9].

In 1964 the Labour government intended to bring in further legislation making all crofters owner-occupiers on a given day, with compensation paid by the state to landlords. The legislation fell when a General Election was called, and the incoming Conservative government failed to revive it.

Norman Cameron's vigorous employee had the honesty to tell him that the 1955 Crofters' Act made her redundant, and she left Shetland for pastures new. Henceforward he relied increasingly on the solicitor James Tait, of the Lerwick firm Tait and Peterson, whose encyclopaedic knowledge and understanding of crofting law were coupled with both wisdom and integrity. Later, too, David Bogle, of the Edinburgh firm Lindsays WS, steered him unobtrusively in a world whose parameters had become increasingly unfamiliar. Bogle recognised the unworldliness of the Camerons, but was perfectly well aware himself of the practical problems awaiting the next generation.

In 1964 Meg's nephew John Scott took over the tenancy of Maryfield Farm. Three years later, after Norman Cameron's unexpected death, he also assumed ownership of the Garth Estate. Suddenly estate tenants found themselves with a young and practical landlord, with extensive agricultural experience, and no interest in reinforcing outdated social stereotypes. Gardie House became a family house. The Camerons had had no time for such niceties as curtains, cushions or comfortable chairs.

Improvements were gradually put in place; the portraits on the walls began to assume identities and even to smile. The gardens were brought back from the state of dereliction into which they had slumped after wartime productivity.

Gardie needed a lot of looking after – the roof had to be replaced in the 1990s, and ongoing maintenance absorbed much time and energy each winter. But the rewards were great. Slowly the house began to reveal its secrets to increasingly fascinated owners, and the sense of continuance, in a society where continuance has, until possibly now, been real, and prized, was a privilege and a reassurance.

The story of Gardie House shows people reacting to the different situations that faced them – some well, some not so well. It seems easy to judge with the benefit of hindsight, as this generation of Shetlanders will no doubt be judged one day. The decision that Magnus Henderson made, not so much to build a house – there was plenty of that happening in his time, as there is now – but to build a house of such sophistication, is still an astonishing one, and his personality remains sufficiently obscure that his motivation – certainly a complex one – is hard to disentangle.

Perhaps however it illustrates one of the enduring interests about Shetland – that this small group of Atlantic islands has produced, and continues to produce, men and women of ability who respond with decision to their environment. Some of them have entered, sometimes briefly, into this story, but there are many more. Human nature does not change. It is plain that the drive and determination necessary to build an enterprise is present in modern Shetland as it was formerly. It is one of the factors which have enabled the islands to survive difficulties and challenges with such a strong and enduring sense of self. The islands remain, casting their subtle spell on the men and women who came here as much as to those who were born here

NOTES:

1   The late Mrs Jeannie Hardie, Hunchibanks, Bressay, to author, pers com.
2   Hance Smith, *Shetland Life and Trade*.
3   The baby duly arrived on St Andrew's Day, 1936. It proved to be a boy, John.
4   Mrs Ella Sutherland, Gunnista, Bressay, pers com. The teak gates are still in use.
5   Annie Kirkpatrick of Slukka, Bressay.
6   This was W.R.T. Hamilton (1905-1997) who, fighting with the New Zealanders, was taken prisoner in Greece, and spent the rest of the war in captivity. He went on to play an active role in Shetland public life; among other offices, he became County Convenor and chairman of Lerwick Harbour Trust. More importantly, he had a warm heart and a generous spirit.
7   Barbara Pitcairn claimed to be the wife, by a secret marriage, of John Gifford, heir to the Busta estate, who was drowned in 1748. His posthumous child Gideon inherited, but Gideon's equivocal status plunged the estate into litigation and bankruptcy.
8   Annsbrae, one of Shetland's historic houses, is today a Listed Building.
9   James Shaw Grant, then Chairman of the Crofters Commission, told John Scott in 1965 that the Bressay holdings were not reorganised because the Fetlar scheme had not worked.

Gardie House publicity drawing when the gardens were opened for charity in the 1990s.   (by Mike Finnie for the Belmont Trust)

ACKNOWLEDGEMENTS

I should like to thank Barbara Anderson, L. F. Anderson, Alan Beattie, the Bressay History Group, J.R.Coull, Andy Duffus, Wendy Gear, Macaulay Hamilton, Brian and Margaret Hunter, John Hunter, George Jamieson, Ian Merrall, Jennifer Roberts (nee Cameron), Duncan and Jan Sandison, Brian Smith and Angus Johnson at the Shetland Archive, Douglas Garden at the Shetland Library, Tommy Watt and Ian Tait at the Shetland Museum, the Unst History Group.

Brian Smith, W.P.L. Thomson, Professor T.C. Smout, Kirsty Hallett and Alec Scott read drafts of the book and I thank them all for their comments and suggestions. It remains true, however, that the responsibility for any errors or omissions rests entirely with me.

Mike Finnie has most generously allowed me to use his lovely line drawings, and done one specially for the book; they are a particular delight and I thank him very much.

I am very particularly indebted to Jane Manson, without whose meticulous work on the Gardie House Archive much of the material used in the book would have remained inaccessible. I thank her too for allowing me to use her own research into 18th and 19th century Bressay, for her help and support through many travails both logistical and technical, and for her companionship on what has been a journey of discovery into the past.

Lastly I thank my family for their encouragement, including my helpful granddaughter Lorna and my daughter Kirsty, supportive from the start; and my husband John, for everything.

Wendy Scott.
Keldabister Banks.

Sources

Most quotations are from documents in the Gardie House Archive (GHA). Where no specific reference is given, the date will act as marker. Some references are from material in the Shetland Archive (SA). Illustrations, where not credited, are the property of the Gardie Trust.

Bibliography

Allan, David – *Scotland in the Eighteenth Century*, Pearson Education, London, 2000.

Ballantyne, John H. and Brian Smith Eds – *Shetland Documents 1195-1879*, Shetland Islands Council and The Shetland Times Ltd, Lerwick, 1999; *Shetland Documents 1580-1611*, Shetland Islands Council and The Shetland Times Ltd, Lerwick, 1994.

Brand, Reverend John – *A Brief Description of Orkney, Zetland, Pightland-Firth and Caithness*, Edinbugh 1701.

Catton, Reverend James – *The History and Description of the Shetland Islands*, Wainfleet, 1838.

Clark, W. Fordyce – *The Story of Shetland*, Oliver and Boyd, Edinburgh 1906.

Cooke, A. and Donnachie, Ian, MacSween, Ann, Whatley, C.A., eds – *Modern Scottish History Vol 1, the Transformation of Scotland 1707-1850*, Tuckwell Press, East Linton, 1998.

Cowie, Robert – *Shetland Descriptive and Historical*, John Menzies and Co, Edinburgh 1874.

Devine, T.M. and Mitchison, Rosalind, Eds – *People and Society in Scotland 1760-1830*, John Donald, Edinburgh 1988.

Devine, T.M. – *The Scottish Nation 1700-2000*. Allan lane, London, 1999; *The Transformation of Rural Scotland 1660-1815*, John Tonald, Edinburgh 1994.

Donaldson, Gordon Ed – *The Court Book of Shetland 1615-1629* Shetland Library, Lerwick, 1991.

Fagon, Brian – *The Little Ice Age, How Climate Made History 1300-1850* Basic Books, New York, 2000.

Fenton, Alexander – *The Northern Isles*, John Donald, Edinburgh, 1978.

Ferguson, William – *Scotland 1689 to the Present*, The Edinburgh History of Scotland, Volume 4, Mercat Press, Edinburgh 1968.

Gear, Wendy – *John Walker's Shetland*, The Shetland Times, Lerwick, 2005.

Graham, Henry Grey – *The Social Life of Scotland in the 18th Century*, A&C Black Ltd, London 1928.

Grant, F.J. – *Zetland Family Histories* T&J Manson, Lerwick, 1907.

Harper, Marjory – *Adventures and Exiles*, Profile Books, London 2003.

Hibbert, Samuel – *A Description of the Shetland Islands*, Edinburgh 1822 (reprinted T&J Manson, Lerwick, 1891).

Knox, Susan A. – *The Making of the Shetland Landscape*, John Donald, Edinburgh, 1985.

Low, Reverend George – *A Tour Through the Islands of Orkney and Schetland*, W. Peace & Son, Kirkwall 1879.

Lynch, Michael – *Scotland, a New History*, Pimlico, London, 1992.

Mitchison, Rosalind – *Lordship to Patronage, Scotland 1603-1745*, Edinburgh University Press, Edinburgh, 1983; *Agricultural Sir John: A Life of Sir John Sinclair of Ulbster, 1754-1835*, Geoffrey Bles, London, 1962.

Peterkin, Alexander – *Notes on Orkney and Zetland*, John Moir, Edinburgh, 1822.

Plant, Marjorie – *The Domestic Life of Scotland in the Eighteenth Century*, Edinburgh University Press, Edinburgh, 1952.

Shaw, Frances J. – *The Northern and Western Islands of Scotland, Their Economy and Society in the Seventeenth Century*, John Donald, Edinburgh, 1980.

Sinclair, Sir John, Ed – *Statistical Account of Scotland 1799 Volume XIX*, introduction Thomas and Graham.

Smith, Brian – *Toons and Tenants*, The Shetland Times Ltd, Lerwick, 2000.

Smith, Hance – *Shetland Life and Trade 1550-1914*, John Donald, Edinburgh, 1984.

Smout, T.C. – *A History of the Scottish People 1560-1830*, Collins, London, 1969.

Tudor, J.R. – *The Orkneys and Shetland: Their Past and Present State*, Stanford, London, 1883.

Waugh, Doreen, Ed – *Shetland's Northern Links, Language and History*, Scottish School for Northern Studies, Lerwick, 1996.

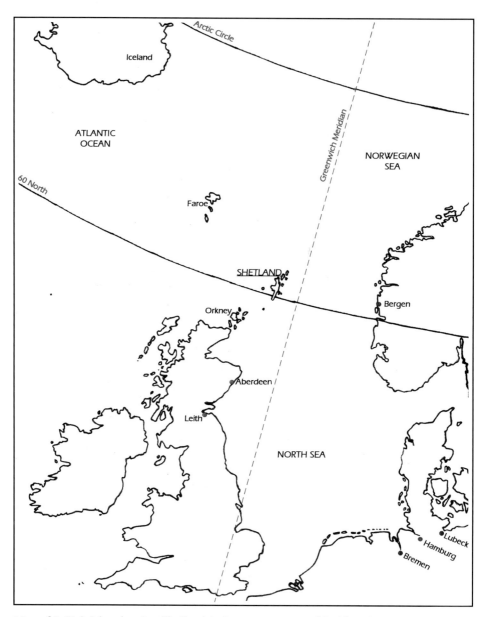

Map of British Isles showing Shetland in its correct geographical location.

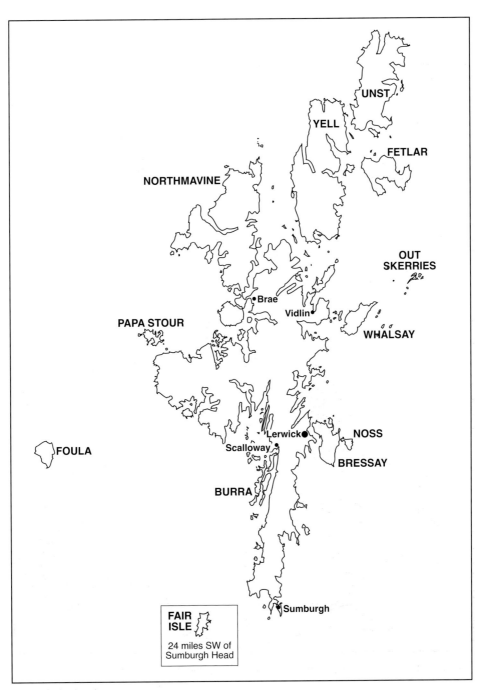

Map of Shetland.

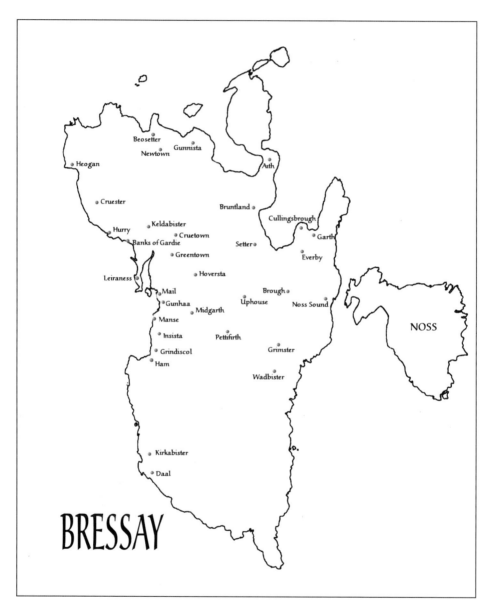

Map of Bressay showing historical places.

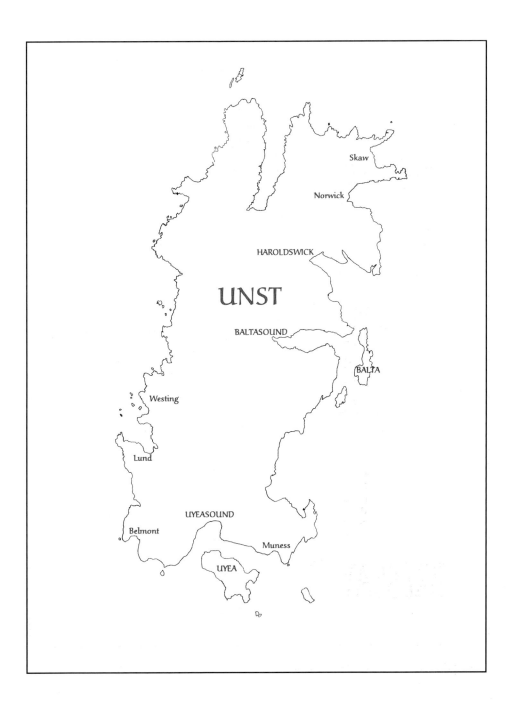

UNST

Skaw

Norwick

HAROLDSWICK

BALTASOUND

BALTA

Westing

Lund

UYEASOUND

Belmont

Muness

UYEA

INDEX

Mitchell, James, (Girlsta) 11,17,19,26
Mouat, Miss Anne *see* Cameron
Mouat, Eliza *see* Cunningham
Mouat, John, Annsbrae 49,51,58,65,71,77
Mouat, Margaret, later Cameron 76,84,86,89,96,105,110,130,132
Mouat, Thomas of Garth 29,**41-49**,64,65,96
Mouat, William, elder 8,29,30,32,41
Mouat, William of Gardie 49,51,**61-80**,84,88,97,99,113,157
Mouat, William Mouat Cameron *see* Cameron

Neven, John 6,8,47
Nicolson, Arthur, (Lochend) 13,23,40
Nicolson, Arthur of Lochend 29
Nicolson, Elizabeth 15,41,42,44,46,49,96
Nicolson, John 20
Nicolson, William of Lochend 11,26

Penney, Thomas 100,116
Penney, William 125,130
Phin, John **85-90**, 96,99,127,128
Pitcairn, George, Muness 19
Pole, William 124

Queen Victoria 159,160

Robertson, Walter 20,21
Rose, Jean 29
Roy, Alan **167-172**

Sandison, Alexander 124,128,129,151
Sandison, Peter 125,126
Scott, Basil, Voesgarth 29
Scott, Hector of Scottshall 11,20
Scott, John H. 183
Scott, Margaret W. **173-179**,
Scott, Sir Walter 75
Spence, Dr William 77,91,
Spence, William of Midyell 8,28

Walker, John **113-136**,146
Williamson, Henry **168-172**
Williamson, Laurence, "Skipper" 2